ANNEX

Labor in the
PHILIPPINE
ECONOMY

Photo by Fenno Jacobs, from Three Lions

Felling a tree on Negros Occidental. The staging on which the men work is built of single bamboo poles held together by rattan.

Kenneth K. Kurihara

Labor in the
PHILIPPINE
ECONOMY

Issued under the Auspices of
American Council
Institute of Pacific Relations

STANFORD UNIVERSITY PRESS
Stanford University, California
London: Geoffrey Cumberlege, Oxford University Press

FOREWORD

The present study is one of several initiated by the Institute of Pacific Relations to explore labor conditions and the state of social welfare in Southeast Asia. The economy of that region is in transition. Its large-scale enterprises, and many of its lesser industries, too, are geared to world trade; but the great majority of the people still are engaged in traditional occupations geared to home consumption and local trade. Wage labor is marginal in the native economy. The laborer who works for wages is essentially a peasant. He looks upon the sale of his labor as an expedient rather than a lifelong vocation. Sometimes he works intermittently for others and hardly distinguishes between an agreed recompense and the present which under local custom he is entitled to expect from a wealthier neighbor when helping him out at certain seasons. Often, he has no land of his own or is the son of a peasant whose holding is too small to keep all his family occupied the year around. When he serves in a small enterprise, rural or industrial, this peasant-laborer still thinks of himself as a servant even when his function has become specialized as that of a producer. Not only is he likely to be unconscious of belonging to a special class, but his employer keeps up the semblance of a household relationship in which the laborer's position may not be very different from that of a poor neighbor or relative. When he serves in a larger undertaking, the laborer usually is one of a crew, and the foreman assumes the function of the paternal employer—"paternal," of course, in the Oriental sense of the word which concedes full authority to the head of the family and exacts complete obedience from the others.

This paternalism, in both instances, verges on tyranny

when the potential labor supply, as often happens, is drawn from a large area and is virtually inexhaustible. In such a case, the moderation forced by public opinion on a local employer in his exploitation of his workers tends to give way to a more impersonal attitude on his part toward his employees, even when these in their simplicity still cherish the old feeling of loyalty toward him. The worst labor conditions in Asia tend to occur in this twilight zone between traditional and modern enterprise. When the workers themselves become aware of the change in their position, their attitude changes. Actually the conditions of their employment may not be inferior to those which they previously experienced as tenant farmers, as sharecroppers, or as employees in small enterprises of the traditional type. But with the breakdown of the native pattern of labor relations a new class-consciousness appears: willing subordination gives way to a sense of conflicting interest.

To the non-Asiatic world this social by-product of modernization has special significance. Thus far, the European or American breadwinner has been content to benefit from the use of cheap labor in the Asiatic tropics. It provided him with inexpensive enrichments of his diet, with a variety of useful articles made by hand labor of tropical materials, and, above all, with raw materials which he could transform with the aid of machinery into a multitude of manufactured commodities. Organized labor was quick to spot the competition of cheap Oriental labor only when it was employed on the production of commodities that could be substituted for those of the industrial West. It did not protest against the exploitation of colored labor when it supplied commodities for direct consumption.

In many countries organized labor tried to protect itself against "unfair Oriental competition" by supporting the movement for higher tariffs, but failed to perceive all the consequences of this mode of action. Living costs tended to rise and real wages to decline. More important, every reduction of imports from the low-wage countries retarded that rise in the purchasing power of peasant-labor populations which offered the largest potential area for the expansion of the world market for manufactured goods. With the growth of the instruments for mass production during the second World War in such countries as the United States, Canada, and Great Britain, the need for larger Oriental markets for their manufactures will be even greater in the years to come. The Asiatic worker's purchasing power, the conditions under which he toils, will at last receive world-wide attention, and this even if it should appear that the immediate need of the East is for such producer goods as the West can provide rather than consumer goods.

In such a region as Southeast Asia, the effects of undeveloped labor standards in modern enterprises are, of course, very different from those in the traditional crafts. To be sure, with modern commercial facilities not only mass products enter the world market but also the products of millions of workers who are employed in small shops and in small rural enterprises. Many of those whose handiwork is lifted by huge steel cranes into vessels of the most modern construction are wholly unacquainted with power-driven machinery. But the greatest danger to Western labor standards comes from the competition of sweated Asiatic labor when it is engaged in operations with modern tools and with power, or when it is set to work in large plants to reproduce in clumsy, out-dated fashion commodities manufactured elsewhere by modern means. It was this type of competition—cheap labor, cheaply housed and implemented, but organized for modern trade—that gave Japanese export trade an edge over that of Western countries in many parts of the world. There is reason to fear that this kind of competition will recur as, one after another, the peoples of tropical Asia, living as yet for the most part in an agricultural and household economy, are drawn into industrial production for the world market.

Every technical improvement increases this potential competition unless there is a corresponding leveling up of labor
standards and unless the millions of workers engaged in
these industries are enabled to consume far larger shares
of the commodities they produce and of others similarly
produced elsewhere.

For this reason if for no other the future development
of labor standards in the dependent and semidependent
areas of the world has become a matter of world importance. That importance is even greater in relation to those
countries which, like the Philippines, may be expected soon
to enter into an era of political independence, when no metropolitan power will have the right to interfere with their
internal arrangements so as to protect the standards of Occidental workers.

The Philippines occupy a peculiar place in this transi-
tional stage of world competition. A genuine industrial
development was never attempted by the Spaniards. They
perceived there as also in their American dependencies that
it was more economical to have some of the local materials
worked up into finished products by native hand labor
rather than to have them shipped in their raw state to be
manufactured by more expensive labor in the home country. But it did not occur to them to make Filipino labor
more productive by an intensification of the capital investment. Even under the American regime, industrialization
proceeded slowly. When the United States became a colonial power, the influence of the industrialists on legislation
was great enough to prevent a serious competition of colonial industries, especially of those offering finished consumer goods. Nevertheless, it was possible for Filipino
labor to benefit from association with rich America. The
raw materials, the food, and the semimanufactured commodities which it could supply enjoyed an assured, and in
some instances a protected, market.

Compared with labor conditions in most of Southeast

Asia, those in the Philippines are already far advanced on the road to modernization. But this does not mean that they provide a model. Quite the contrary. The Philippine Government and other leaders in Philippine social life are only too well aware how much still remains to be done to provide even a minimum of security and worth-while existence to the Islands' laboring masses. They also know that their country, situated as it is in the tropics, with all their limiting climatic and historical factors, may never experience a full-blown "Industrial Revolution." At any rate, thoughtful Filipinos realize that for many generations they will have to seek the highest type of life and culture attainable within the frame of a mixed economy, still largely controlled by pre-industrial traditions. It is for such a society that they must plan.

The completion of the Philippines' political emancipation is an important element in the improvement of the country's labor conditions, but not the most important. The United States government has, in recent times, exerted little if any influence on Philippine domestic legislation. And there is no sign that American enterprise or the investment of American capital in Philippine industry will be greatly affected by the political change. The greatest impediment to progress is the relative slowness of social change in the Islands as compared with that of political change. Outwardly conforming to a democratic form of government, Philippine society still is in the main ruled by an oligarchy. The Philippine Government will continue to be handicapped by the same privileged interests and reactionary forces which have made the path of welfare legislation and administration so steep and stony in the past. The progressive forces in the Islands will need the support of an informed world opinion if the new problems in labor relations that have already begun to arise from the general economic situation since the end of the war are to be solved with practical statesmanship.

The techniques of international study, discussion, and agreement, once more exemplified in 1944 and 1945 at the twenty-sixth and twenty-seventh sessions of the International Labor Conference, can be used to strengthen the hands of the Philippine Government in this matter. For, while it is impossible for an international body to legislate successfully on labor situations that differ so greatly from country to country, the level of achievement in the Philippines still is so low in many respects that even the application of agreed minimum standards would represent substantial advances. Large numbers of Filipino wage-earners and share-croppers are not yet secure in the possession of any of the "freedoms," the establishment of which is among the peace aims of the United Nations. Labor is for the most part unorganized and unrepresented. The government of President Quezon was sympathetic to the aspirations of all those who work for their living, but it was not able to win for its enlightened policies a majority of those who wield economic power.

The present study is offered, then, as a description of a situation in flux, a situation burdened with a heavy heritage of unresolved problems and grievances, yet hopeful in that the directions leading toward higher labor standards are clear and the forces working in those directions impressive. The findings should not be regarded as "typical" for dependent territories or for Southeast Asia. Nor may they serve as models. Part way between a pre-industrial pattern of economic society and a truly rationalized modern pattern, Philippine industrial society has reached a stage, rather, which other parts of tropical Asia may reach later if present plans for their industrialization should mature.

The author has studied labor conditions in the Philippines at first hand as a lecturer in Economics at the University of the Philippines. He is a graduate of Iowa State University and of Yale University. Responsibility for the

facts and opinions stated in the text rests entirely with the
author and not with the Institute of Pacific Relations whose
American Council, nevertheless, has pleasure in offering
this study as a contribution to the knowledge of labor conditions in the Pacific area.

BRUNO LASKER

NEW YORK
November 1945

CONTENTS

LIST OF TABLES

LIST OF ILLUSTRATIONS

INTRODUCTION

On December 8, 1941, war came to the Philippines, without provocation and almost without warning. The war brought about economic dislocations and at once disrupted the program leading to the independence of the Islands in 1946. The national economy of the Philippines had to be geared to a wartime economy. All the available resources of the country had to be reallocated to satisfy the military requirements. Reference will be made later to the possible effects of Japanese occupation—effects which cannot yet be fully recognized. Suffice it to say here that, in its utilization of the country's resources, the occupying power allowed military expediency to outweigh any considerations of the welfare of Filipinos.

Most relevant to the matter in hand is the sudden interruption of the "Social Justice" program of the Commonwealth Government. The working class had just begun to get the feel of the program developed under that policy when the war cut it short. One of the big jobs of the postwar period will be to revitalize the labor movement; for it is vital to the country's social progress and economic welfare. It is necessary, therefore, to examine the role which organized labor will be likely to play in the postwar economic reconstruction of the country.

Although labor problems press for solution in the Philippines, there are only scattered and isolated data on their character and origin. Labor conditions have been described as though divorced from economic history. This circumstance explains the purpose of the present study; namely, to show the development of Philippine labor problems against the background of the national economy. Incidentally this study may also help to provide a theoretical basis for progressive labor policies.

The material of this work dates mostly from the pre-war period. The study is handicapped by the lack of important data in the United States and by the fact that in many instances the author has had to rely on secondary sources.

The general setting need be recalled here only in brief-est outline. The Commonwealth of the Philippines is a country larger than Italy and a little smaller than the British Isles. It exceeds the combined areas of the states of New York, New Jersey, Pennsylvania, and Delaware. Its population, 17,000,000, is larger than the combined populations of Norway, Sweden, and Denmark, and is about one-fifth that of Japan.

There are 7,100 islands in the archipelago, but only thirty of these are each more than 100 square miles in extent. In the north is the largest island, Luzon (40,420 square miles). The next largest is Mindanao in the south-east (36,537 square miles). Between Luzon and Mindanao is a group of islands called the Visayas, the largest of which are Samar, Negros, Panay, Leyte, Cebu, and Bohol. In the west lie a long narrow island called Palawan and the Calamian Islands. The total area of the Philippines is 115,600 square miles. The distance from the northern to the southern extremity is about 1,120 miles, or a little more than that from Washington, D.C., to Kansas City.

The southernmost parts of the Philippines are about five degrees north of the Equator; and the climate of the islands is tropical, with an average temperature of about 80°. The term "tropical," however, includes a great vari-ety of conditions. For example, on the western slopes of the islands bisected by a high cordillera there is a pro-nounced dry season which lasts from November to May, April and May being the hottest months, and a wet season from June to October. In the Cagayan Valley of Luzon and on parts of the eastern coast the distribution of the seasons is quite different, and they are less sharply contrasted. Generally speaking, the eastern coasts of the islands have rainfall the year around; this leaches the soil and makes it less favorable for agriculture. As a result, most of the important economic developments have taken place on the western side, where there is a pronounced seasonal rhythm.

I
NATURE OF THE PHILIPPINE LABOR PROBLEM

Labor problems in the Philippines are superficially the same as those in other capitalistic countries. However, there is one important difference: Philippine labor problems are complicated by political problems peculiar to a subject country. They have more in common with those of British India, Korea, the Netherlands East Indies, French Indo-China, and other dependencies than with those of industrialized, independent countries. In all these colonial and semicolonial countries the problems of industrial workers are overshadowed by those of peasants, tenant farmers, and farm hands.

Backward Agrarian Economy

Philippine labor problems are products of a colonial agrarian economy. As such, they are tied with the whole social and political development of the country. They combine the problems of rural workers bound to the soil and those of modern wage earners. The so-called "agrarian question" occupies the forefront of labor struggles in the Philippines. For purposes of analysis, the specific problems of the rural workers may be separated from those of the urban proletariat; but in reality they have a certain unity of meaning and import. In a country like the United States, the interests of farmers are often in conflict with those of urban workers: the former, living largely on their own produce, are interested in high prices; the latter, having to buy what they consume, are more interested in low grocery bills. On the other hand, in the Philippines, where the overwhelming majority of the working population consists of peasants, small tenants, and farm hands, the "country folks" and the "city folks" see eye to eye on many questions. Hence there is no such thing in the Philippines as a "farmer movement" independent of and distinct from "the labor movement." In fact, peasant organizations and trade-unions frequently form a common united front.

The most obvious, yet often disregarded, fact about the Philippine economy is that it is predominantly agricultural. Agriculture provided a living for 65 per cent of the gainfully employed workers according to the 1939 *Census of the Philippines.*[1] In 1939 the Philippine Department of Agriculture and Commerce reported that agricultural products accounted for about four-fifths of the total exports from the Philippines.[2] The relative importance of agriculture is reflected also in the sources of Philippine national income listed in Table I.

TABLE I

SOURCES OF NATIONAL INCOME, 1939*

	Percentage		Percentage
Agriculture	56.80	Fisheries	13.35
Livestock	1.75	Mining	8.27
Industry	14.50	Forestry	5.33

* Compilation by the Royal Institute of International Affairs, "The Philippines in Transition," *Bulletin of International News*, August 23, 1941.

Yet, technically, agriculture lags far behind industry in the Philippines and still shows traces of feudalism. While the industrial centers have put on a semblance of modern life, the countryside is characterized today by pretty much the same primitive life as under the Spanish regime. During that regime native agriculture and industry were more or less neglected by the colonial officials, who were reaping great profits from the galleon trade. After the American occupation, native agriculture became adapted to the peculiar marketing conditions that resulted from the new political affiliation. The dominating influence on the selection of commercial crops was not, as theoretically

[1] Volume II, p. 484.
[2] *Facts and Figures about the Philippines* (Manila, 1939).

might have been expected, the actual industrial requirements of the American economy, but the tariff.

High tariff rates, intended to discourage importation in competition with American production, had the reverse effect in the Philippines when the exports of that country were permitted to flow freely toward the otherwise highly protected continental market. Attracted by prices boosted higher and higher with each succeeding tariff, the Philippine producers specialized in precisely those of their potential export commodities which the Congressional friends of the American farmer had tried to keep out. Shipments of sugar, coconut, abaca, tobacco, and other crops from the Philippines to continental United States directly or indirectly in competition with America's tariff-protected commercial crops, became ever larger. Other tropical agricultural industries which might have had fair market prospects in other parts of the world but which did not feel the stimulus of the artificially raised American prices were neglected, and some of them remain to this day in a pre-capitalistic and pre-industrial state of production exclusively for domestic use.

When serfdom was abolished by Spanish legislation, a substitute system was introduced in the Philippines, with the result that the legally emancipated serfs remained attached to the soil. This substitute is what is today known as the *kasama* system. Under this system the landlord and the tenant share the cost of production and the produce on a fifty-fifty basis; or in some cases the landlord's share, especially of the products, may run as high as two-thirds of the total. The actual tenure of this system differs from province to province, but in all cases the tenants are sharecroppers. Under the *hacienda* system, some laborers are hired to work for wages. This system prevails in sugar plantations but is less developed than the other because tenant labor is still the most profitable source of income for the landowners.

Usury persists in spite of the anti-usury law. Customary rates of interest on loans, whether in cash or in produce, range from 30 to 100 per cent for half a year. Tenants are often ignorant of their legal rights and are drawn into debt through intimidation. It was partly for the purpose of remedying this situation that the government in August 1939 established an Agricultural and Industrial Bank to make credit available to small farmers on cheap and easy terms.

The extreme concentration of land ownership also is a remnant of Spanish times. As late as 1898 the Recollects, Dominicans, and Augustinians were reported as owning 420,000 acres, including some of the best land in the Philippines.[3] It was partly to alter this that the revolution of 1896 had been directed. Yet the Dominican friars still owned the Buenavista estate of 27,400 hectares when in 1939 the government leased it for a co-operative experiment.

An example of great inequality in land distribution in the Philippines is furnished by the latest census figures: less than one per cent of Pampanga's population own that province's 120,715 hectares of agricultural lands; and only 12.5 per cent of its 23,628 farmers own all the land they cultivate.[4] The large landed estates are commonly regarded as the greatest single cause of agrarian trouble in the Philippines.

The capitalistic method of production has not yet penetrated deeply into Philippine agriculture. The Socialist leader, Pedro Abad Santos, has been reported as saying: "What we need in this country right now is more capitalism." Backward agriculture has a retarding effect on the labor movement. With the preponderance of agricultural as opposed to industrial labor go the difficulties of working-

[3] *Cf.*, Pilar B. Garces, *The Agrarian Convicts in Bulacan* (unpublished Master's thesis, Far Eastern University, Manila, 1937).

[4] *Census of the Philippines*, 1939, Vol. III, p. 1396.

class organization. Any study of organized labor in the
Philippines deals with only a comparatively small section
of the working population.

Slow Industrial Development

Philippine industry as a whole has not yet outgrown
the handicraft stage. Most of the country's industrial output still comes from the home or from small workshops
and is produced under the old forms of organization.
According to the 1918 *Census* there were in the Philippines
8,500 "industries."[5] In 1938 the Department of Agriculture and Commerce estimated the number of industrial
firms in Manila at 550.[6] In these days of corporate organization it is not, however, the number of independent
industrial firms but the scale of operation that counts. At
any rate, mass production on a nation-wide basis is yet
to come.

Although before 1942 industry was beginning to occupy
an increasingly important place in the national economy,
its development had been slow for many interrelated
reasons. There was hardly any constructive effort and
encouragement to develop industry during the Spanish
regime, which was purely colonial. Later, free trade with
the United States also had the effect of retarding the growth
of native industry; for the United States could supply not
only production goods but also consumption goods in
exchange for tropical products and other Philippine raw
materials. The natural tendency was for only the export
industries to be given inducement for development, and
most of the capital investment went into that field. Thus,
under American as under Spanish rule the Philippines
remained a raw-material appendage of the industrial economy of the mother country. This applies to the present

[5] No comparable figures have been compiled from the 1939 *Census*.
[6] *Manila Bulletin*, June 20, 1938.

status of Philippine industry under temporary Japanese control.[7]

Industrial backwardness accounted for some of the principal imports of the Philippines, such as iron and steel products, cotton and rayon textiles, machinery and parts, automobiles and trucks, paper and paper products, and chemicals and fertilizer. The major exports of the country were raw materials and unfinished goods, such as sugar, copra, abaca, tobacco, timber, coconut oil, and semi-refined gold bullion. Economic dependence on the United States thus largely accounted for the immature growth of native industry.

Miss Catherine Porter, who made a personal investigation of Philippine industry, observed:

> The backbone of the country's industry [in 1918] was the little home shops in which all kinds of materials were worked and a wide variety of products offered for local consumption and in a few cases for export. Since then, there has been a concentration of industry about the agricultural export crops, at the expense of some of the home industries, but very little large-scale organization of manufacturing such as is common in Western countries, in Japan, and in the coast cities of China.[8]

Thus the foreground of the Philippine industrial fabric was occupied by prosperous, large, modern export enterprises. This picture cannot have changed materially during the Japanese occupation. Backward industry is even more detrimental to the interests of labor than is backward agriculture, for the bargaining strength of organized labor lies in a widespread factory system. Labor organization will be strengthened to the precise degree that the country becomes industrialized.

----

[7] According to a *Domei* broadcast of March 15, 1943, a "five-year plan" had been adopted by Tokyo's Philippine Executive Committee in order to increase, with forced Filipino labor, the production of rice, potatoes, beans, corn, and other staple foods.

[8] *Far Eastern Survey*, June 29, 1938, p. 144.

Control of Industry

Many, though not all, of the country's modern industries and commercial developments, financed with outside capital, have been controlled by non-Filipinos. Since they were, on the whole, more efficiently organized and run than the more traditional trades which remained in Filipino hands, a large part of the profits obviously benefited American and foreign rather than indigenous owners. In this matter, Philippine experience was no different from that in European dependencies or in independent countries which, economically, occupy a semi-colonial status. The only difference, perhaps, was that Americans were more willing to plow earnings back again into the industries they owned with a view to further large developments; naturally they played the leading role, with Spanish, British, Chinese, Japanese, and other foreign enterprises following in that order.

All the prerequisites of safe and profitable investment were present in the Philippines: cheap labor, cheap but fertile land, cheap raw materials, low taxes, and a measure of political stability. To the extent to which capital seeks a profitable field of investment anywhere, irrespective of national barriers, it tends to flow into backward, undeveloped areas where the rate of return is high and where prospects of continuing enterprises are good. The Philippines were just such a country.

The American investment in the Islands before the war was about a fifth of the total investment. According to a survey, made by the United States Department of Commerce, of direct American investments in foreign countries at the end of 1936, the investment in the Philippines stood at $92,000,000, while American investments in China amounted to $91,000,000 and those in the Netherlands East Indies were estimated at $70,000,000.[9] Outside capi-

[9] Paul D. Dickens, *American Direct Investments in Foreign Countries, 1936.* United States Dept. of Commerce, Bureau of Foreign and Domestic Commerce, Economic Series No. 1, pp. 16–17.

tal also dominated banking and public utilities in the Philippines. Sugar production was controlled largely by American and Spanish capital. Gold, iron ore, and chromite production was controlled largely by American capital. Coconut oil was controlled largely by American and to a certain extent by British capital. Spanish interests dominated the tobacco industry. Half of the investment in the cordage industry was American, the other half Spanish. Chinese capital dominated the timber and lumber industry. Chinese and Japanese together controlled about two-thirds of the retail trade.

Thus the key enterprises were either controlled or owned by American and foreign capital. No wonder that there was so much agitation for the "Filipinization" of industry in the Philippines. Many Filipino workers and peasants, especially those belonging to organized labor, thought they were toiling to earn profit, dividend, rent, and interest largely for "foreign" investors. Thoughtful Filipinos were apprehensive especially of the political implications of non-American foreign-capital investments in their country, fearing that foreign capital might serve as the spearhead of political aggrandizement. They were especially sensitive to Japanese economic penetration. For example, at a discussion held in 1938 by the Philippine Council of the Institute of Pacific Relations, Professor José Apostol of the College of Business Administration, University of the Philippines, asked if so-called "peaceful penetration" did not mean "the process of acquiring economic interests as a basis for political penetration," and asked if this was not the case with Japanese economic interests in the Philippines.[10]

Various measures were taken to counteract such foreign economic control or to arrest further foreign economic penetration. Article XII, Section I, of the Philippine Con-

[10] Philippine Council, Institute of Pacific Relations, *Some Philippine Points of View of the Sino-Japanese Situation* (Manila, March 1938).

stitution provides that no corporations for the operation of
public utilities, mining, and the exploitation of other natural
resources may have less than 60 per cent Filipino or American capital. Yet time and again foreign capital was able
to get around this provision by means of "dummies," although the Public Service Commission, the Securities and
Exchange Commission, the Bureau of Banking, and other
government agencies did their best to prevent undue foreign
economic control. The land and fishing laws also provide
for the protection of the patrimony of the Filipino people.
There was, before the war, a movement to limit the issuance
of trade and professional licenses to alien applicants. And
there were other legislative and legal moves toward arrest-
ing foreign control. There was a growing realization among
the leaders that the country's natural resources must be
utilized by Filipinos for Filipinos.

The Philippines offered at the same time a rich source
of raw materials, a profitable field of investment, and a
substantial market; hence the dilemma: "too rich to be
dependent and too poor to be independent." This potentially rich country was too much of a temptation to be
left alone, yet its actual poverty demanded continued
American protection, both political and economic. The
economic nationalism that was current before the war
attempted to solve this dilemma.

Despite all the efforts to arrest outside economic control and to attain economic self sufficiency, American and
foreign investment, both direct and indirect, will continue
as the industrialization of the country proceeds. Industrially the Philippines are still in the "borrowing stage," as
evidenced by the large amount of interest, dividends, and
rent they must pay to outside investors. These payments in
the past have constituted large invisible items in Philippine
foreign trade, and have served to some degree to offset the
"favorable" balance of trade.[11]

[11] Considering all items, visible and invisible, the balance since 1921,

The postwar economic reconstruction of the country will doubtless require more borrowing from abroad. Increased capital investments of outsiders in the Philippines would be a great material advantage to the country if no imperialistic string were attached to them. Moreover, as will be shown below, outside investors probably would be economically benefited if they were to attach more weight to the material welfare of the Filipino people than to immediate profits; for the working efficiency of the Filipino laborer is not yet by any means as high as it might be. Unless he notices signs of such concern, it is cold comfort for the Filipino worker to know that "in the long run" outside investment will benefit all concerned. Since investment—American, foreign, or native—is functionally related to national output, income, and employment, its effective control must remain a matter of great importance to the Filipino people.

Population and Labor Supply

According to the 1939 *Census* the total population of the Philippines was 16,000,303, consisting of 15,833,649 Filipinos, 117,487 Chinese, 29,057 Japanese, 8,709 Americans, 4,627 Spaniards, and 6,774 other foreign residents. At the time of the Spanish occupation, in the latter part of the sixteenth century, the population of the Islands was estimated at half a million. The first census after the American occupation recorded a population of 7,635,426. Fifteen years later—that is, in 1918—the number had increased to 10,314,310. Thus by 1939, after some forty years of the American regime, the Philippine population had doubled.

Perhaps the most important reason for so large a population growth is economic, i.e., greater national output, income, and consumption. However, population has grown

despite these factors, has been highly "favorable" to the Philippines. See *United States Tariff Commission Report No. 118; Fifth and Sixth Annual Reports of the United States High Commissioner to the Philippines.*

Steam-shovel mining on Samar

Underground hand shovelers with Granby car in gold mine at Balatoc
near Baguio

in the Philippines without raising the general plane of living, while in the United States the rate of population growth has declined along with a rise in the plane of living. A large contributing factor in population growth was the introduction and development by the American regime of public hygiene and medical science in the Islands, with a resulting decrease in mortality. The traditional religious (Catholic) opposition to birth control has in this case prevented the usual effect of rising incomes on the birth rate.

The upward trend in population growth was hailed in some quarters as a reflection of national progress. The traditional policy of the Church and the landlords to encourage large families has by no means lost ground. Only small circles of Filipinos are as yet able to weigh the economic consequences of a rapid growth in numbers. The Filipino people will sooner or later be confronted with a choice between reducing the population to the level of the national income and raising national output to the level of population.

Class division is more obvious in the Philippines than in some of the industrialized countries because of the conspicuous absence of a large middle class. In reality there is no such typical Filipino as "Juan de la Cruz," the counterpart of "John Smith." The so-called *tao* approaches this theoretical prototype; he is "the backbone of the country" as well as the main source of the labor supply.

The total number of gainfully employed persons (over ten years of age) in the Philippines before the war was estimated at 5,300,000, or nearly a third of the total population. Table II shows the distribution of the labor supply.

The figures indicate the relative importance of various occupation groups in the national ecenomy of the Philippines. It is important to note that 65 per cent of the gainfully employed workers were engaged in agriculture, while industry proper accounted for only 11.3 per cent. However, this should not be taken to mean that industry is

TABLE II

Gainfully Employed Workers, by Occupation Groups and Sex, 1939*

Occupation Group	Number (Ten years old and over)			Percentage of Distribution			Percentage of Total	
	Both Sexes	Male	Female	Both Sexes	Male	Female	Male	Female
Agriculture	3,456,370	2,981,551	474,819	65.0	70.6	43.2	86.3	13.7
Domestic and personal service[a]	330,764	123,508	207,256	6.2	2.9	18.8	37.3	62.7
Professional service	103,415	65,438	37,977	1.9	1.6	3.5	63.2	36.8
Public service (not elsewhere classified)	49,620	48,984	636	.9	1.2	[b]	98.7	1.3
Fishing	180,569	175,841	4,728	3.5	4.2	.4	97.4	2.6
Forestry and hunting	26,820	24,903	1,917	.5	.6	.2	92.8	7.2
Mining and quarrying	47,019	46,625	394	.9	1.1	[b]	99.2	.8
Manufacturing and mechanical industries	601,335	333,976	267,359	11.3	7.9	24.5	55.6	44.4
Transportation and communication	203,596	202,449	1,147	3.8	4.7	[b]	99.5	.5
Clerical	48,899	44,904	3,995	.9	1.1	.4	91.9	8.1
Trade	270,766	171,099	99,667	5.1	4.1	9.0	63.1	36.9
Total	5,319,173	4,219,278	1,099,895	100.0	100.0	100.0	79.3	20.7

* *Census of the Philippines,* 1939, II, 484, corrected to exclude housewives (see p. 483).

[a] Excluding housewives.

[b] Less than a tenth of one per cent.

proportionally less productive than agriculture. Productivity depends not so much upon the number of workers employed as upon the optimum application of capital to labor. Indicative of the nature and scope of Philippine industry is the distribution of the labor supply, given in Table III.

TABLE III

Workers Engaged in Manufacturing and Mechanical Industries, Arranged in Order of Importance, 1939*

Industry	Number of Workers		
	Both Sexes	Male	Female
Embroidery and dressmaking	113,810	2,630	111,180
Carpentry	76,465	76,457	8
Native textile manufacture	55,834	1,047	54,787

* *Census of the Philippines,* 1939, II, 489.

TABLE III—*Continued*

Industry	Number of Workers		
	Both Sexes	Male	Female
Laborers (industry not stated)..........	51,504	48,300	3,204
Mat manufacture	27,318	1,120	26,198
Tailor shops and necktie manufacture....	23,723	15,729	7,994
Hat manufacture	23,296	2,848	20,448
Sugar centrals and muscovado mills......	22,044	21,762	282
Saw and planing mills..................	21,785	21,747	38
Shoe and slipper manufacture..........	20,271	14,523	5,748
Miscellaneous manufactures	12,281	7,111	5,170
Nipa Manufacture	11,058	5,311	5,747
Cigar and cigarette manufacture........	11,027	5,272	5,755
Bakeries	10,374	9,509	865
Rice and corn mills...................	9,249	7,971	1,278
Garage and auto repair shops..........	7,126	7,116	10
Blacksmith shops	6,892	6,890	2
Clay, brick, tile, and pottery manufacture	6,733	2,307	4,426
Ship and boat manufacture.............	6,226	6,197	29
Building and construction industry.......	6,128	6,122	6
Painting	6,118	6,093	25
Bamboo manufacture	5,274	2,746	2,528
Clock, watch, and jewelry manufacture...	4,749	4,612	137
Desiccated coconut manufacture.........	4,311	3,059	1,252
Printing and publishing................	4,169	3,798	371
Salt manufacture	3,571	2,857	714
Electric plants	3,548	3,548	......
Slaughterhouses	3,532	3,475	57
Furniture manufacture	3,522	3,184	338
Cordage manufacture	2,929	1,419	1,510
Typewriter, radio, and other repairs.....	2,905	2,895	10
Electric light, power, and gas manufacture	2,838	2,811	27
Shirt manufacture	2,492	433	2,059
Plumbing	2,242	2,242	......
Sawali manufacture	2,014	1,113	901
Coconut oil manufacture...............	1,933	1,844	89
Lime and cement manufacture..........	1,687	1,599	88
Candy and caramel manufacture........	1,498	677	821
Hemp mills, abaca stripping and baling..	1,442	1,225	217
Foundries and welding shops...........	1,441	1,438	3
Apa, hopia, and ampaw manufacture....	1,365	384	981
Tinsmith shops	1,251	1,240	11
Bolo, spear, and axe manufacture........	1,139	1,117	22
Fish curing, salting, and drying.........	1,123	867	256
Aerated and distilled water manufacture..	1,063	965	98
Leather products manufacture..........	1,013	918	95

TABLE III—*Concluded*

Industry	Number of Workers		
	Both Sexes	Male	Female
Charcoal manufacture	840	788	52
Carpentry shops	671	654	17
Ice manufacture	634	620	14
Soap manufacture	597	564	33
Match manufacture	546	367	179
Breweries	523	510	13
Button and other shell products manufacture	506	398	108
Sack manufacture	494	126	368
Woodworking and box manufacture.....	473	419	54
Dairy products manufacture............	448	372	76
Broom and brush manufacture..........	353	229	124
Musical instruments manufacture.......	346	289	57
Liquor and beverage manufacture.......	315	309	6
Textile manufacture	311	269	42
Carriage, calesa, and carromata manufacture	289	106	183
Fish and sea products canning..........	252	249	3
Tayo and taho manufacture............	251	195	56
Paper processing	220	196	24
Lithography and engraving............	199	153	46
Candle manufacture	196	187	9
Pineapple canning	179	137	42
Agricultural implements manufacture....	112	77	35
Paint and varnish manufacture.........	95	95	..
Toy manufacture	84	68	16
Fruit and vegetable canning...........	48	42	6
Fertilizer manufacture	25	14	11
Total............................	601,335	333,976	267,359

There is no correlation between the numerical order of importance and the productivity, profitability, or unionization. Take the embroidery and dressmaking industry, for example. More people were employed in this than in any other manufacturing industry, and yet the industry was far less productive, far less profitable, and far less unionized than some of the others employing fewer workers. This particular industry happened to require less fixed capital and more labor. The huge number of female workers in this industry largely accounts for lack of interest in its unionization.

Woman and Child Labor

In the Philippines, as in other countries, the participation of women and minors in various productive activities is traditional, imposed by economic necessity. The relatively high social status and freedom of Filipina women, partly a remnant of the matriarchal customary law which prevailed in pre-Spanish times and partly a result of American influence, enabled an increasing number of women and girls to participate as wage earners in industrial, commercial, and professional fields. The introduction of easily operated machinery made the employment of child labor possible. Insufficient earnings of the main breadwinner often drove wives and children to seek employment, and the employer took advantage of their cheaper labor.

According to the 1939 *Census,* of the total gainfully employed female workers—1,099,895, or 20.7 per cent of the working population—474,819, or 43.2 per cent, were engaged in agriculture, and 267,359, or 24.5 per cent, in manufacturing and mechanical industries. The next largest number of women workers was found in domestic and personal service—207,256, or 18.8 per cent of the total female workers. Only 3.5 per cent of all women workers were in commercial and professional services. These figures reveal the unskilled and backward status of Filipina women workers.

Women workers were paid much less than men for the same work. The textile, embroidery, cigar and cigarette, pottery, shirt, and candy factories and the rice mills have paid especially low wages to their women employees. Average monthly wages for women in these industries were as low as 8, 10, 12, and 14 pesos.[12] Valeria A. Villa, chief

[12] One peso = 100 centavos, equivalent to 50 cents in United States currency.

of the Woman and Child Labor Section of the Bureau of Labor in 1938, said: "The miserable condition of women pieceworkers in some factories is aggravated by the fact that sometimes no work is available for them for a number of days during a week."[13] Those pieceworkers usually worked more than twelve hours a day and raced against time to make their meager earnings. The sweatshop was the rule rather than the exception as far as most female pieceworkers were concerned.

Wages for child workers were even lower. According to the report quoted, the highest weekly wage paid to a minor was ₱7.00, received by a reviser in an embroidery shop; and the lowest was one of ₱1.00 received by a regular child worker in a tobacco factory. Apprentices were paid as little as 45 centavos a week.

Official investigators found that many of the large shoe factories, embroidery houses, cigar and cigarette factories, and perfumeries had installed separate dressing rooms, dining rooms, toilets, and lavatories for women. However, in the majority of the industrial firms employing women and minors no special consideration was given to their convenience and comfort. In agriculture, women and children suffered from the same deplorable working conditions as men. Sanitation, hygiene, medical facilities, safety devices, and other essentials of good working conditions were practically unknown except in a few semi-industrialized lines of work.

There were various legal regulations for the protection of women and minors in industry, but few of these regulations covered the vast number of women and children in domestic service and agriculture. Act No. 3071 regulated "the employment of women and children in shops, factories, industrial, agricultural, and mercantile establishments, and other places of labor in the Philippines." Fourteen was the legal age limit of child labor in dangerous industries and

[13] *Labor Bulletin*, Manila, December 1938.

occupations. In confinement cases, two months' vacation, with pay, was provided for women workers. But the enforcement of these provisions was extremely loose. The exploitation of woman and child labor was made easy in the Philippines by the fact that the overwhelming majority of the adult male workers were ill-paid. An inadequate school system was an additional reason for child labor. Almost every year a "school crisis" occurred in the Philippines, for there were not enough elementary schools to take care of all the school-age children who could afford to go to school.

Conrado Benitez, former Dean of the College of Business Administration, University of the Philippines, estimated the following school attendance "mortality": 58 per cent of the first-grade pupils dropped out after the fourth grade, 86 per cent after the seventh grade, and 97 per cent after the fourth year of high school.[14] The majority of those who dropped out did so for economic reasons. According to the 1939 *Census*, of 1,870,666 children of primary-school age (7 to 10), 773,665, or 41.4 per cent, were attending school; and of 1,347,578 boys and girls between 14 and 17 years of age, 329,628, or 24.5 per cent, were attending classes. Of the 7,460,000 persons 20 years old and over, 62 per cent had not received any schooling. Of those who had attended school, about three-fifths had not completed Grade IV.[15]

Not only have the Philippines the economic problem that arises from the existence of a large child-labor market, but this in turn produces social and political problems. The lot of the illiterate youths, with the exception of a limited number of the more ambitious or more fortunate, is that of common laborers who "stay put" in the lowest wage class. Unless many thousands of children are taken out of the labor market and provided with adequate educational fa-

[14] *Business*, Manila, November 1938. For more educational data, see J. R. Hayden, *The Philippines* (New York, 1941), pp. 471–73.

[15] *Census of the Philippines*, 1939, II, 190 pages.

cilities, they will continue to depress the overcrowded labor market.

Women enjoy a much higher social status in the Philippines than in other Oriental countries. In 1937 they won the right to vote. Yet some elements in the South European attitude toward women, introduced by Spain, still persist. They are as yet far from being socially emancipated in an American sense. Only as they acquire more economic independence will they become freer socially. On the eve of the plebiscite for woman suffrage, a feminist voiced the sentiment of intelligent Filipina women in the following appeal:

So long as women's work is restricted to housekeeping and the rearing of children, so long as they take a minor part in the productive work of society, and remain economically dependent upon men, just so long will they remain subordinate to men in society. It is only when women take an extensive and important part in the productive process of society that they have achieved any rights at all . . . . The economic development of our own country has not yet reached the point at which women take as extensive a part in production as they do in countries more industrially advanced. Therefore our women are still dormant. They are just beginning to hear of "women's rights." Many of them undoubtedly acquiesce in the reactionary notions that women's place is in the home, that feminine charm and virtues will be soiled by the exercise of the right to vote, and that they should remain in the background, deferential. That such objections to woman suffrage only reveal the intellectual backwardness of those who voice them will not be denied by any intelligent person. Of course our women should have the right to vote. Of course they should take part in the political life of the country as much as men do. This right should have been granted by our constitution as a matter of course, and without all this expense of a plebiscite.[16]

[16] Pilar Santa Ana, "The Emancipation of Women," *The National Review*, Manila, March 12, 1937.

Fiber looms, Bureau of Plant Industry, Manila

Photo by Palmer Pictures

Weaving piña cloth. The best piña is woven at Iloilo.

II

THE SOCIAL JUSTICE PROGRAM

In the Philippines, as elsewhere, there had been before the war a growing realization and consciousness, among the progressive elements in particular, that the material and spiritual well-being of the laboring class is a prerequisite to national prosperity and progress. The "Social Justice" program of the Commonwealth Government was a manifestation of this progressive trend. For instance, in 1939, former Secretary of Labor José Avelino emphasized the social significance of labor problems as follows:

> Labor problems demand the attention of all classes of people. The social condition of labor in any country is an index of its progress and civilization. Where labor is neglected and forgotten, that country is decadent and unprogressive. In America, England, France, Russia and other progressive nations, the recognition of labor has accelerated progress. National decadence, chaos, and social discontent are traceable to the oppression and exploitation of the laboring class.[1]

That labor had been "neglected and forgotten" in the Philippines in the past was frankly admitted by national leaders. President Manuel Quezon was quite emphatic on this point when in 1938 he said:

> If my administration is placing special emphasis on the need for ameliorating the conditions of the laboring class, it is not because we are against the capitalists or the rich, but it is because the laboring class in the Philippines has not received its due, and therefore stands in need of the help and protection of the government in order that its rights may be properly recognized and accorded.[2]

Against the background of the depression and general social unrest in the 1930's the Commonwealth Govern-

[1] Speech delivered before a summer convocation at the Far Eastern University, Manila, May 20, 1939.

[2] Message of the President of the Philippines to the National Assembly, February 16, 1938.

23

ment announced a new deal for the working people in the form of the Social Justice program. Probably under the influence of President Roosevelt's "New Deal" and the agrarian reforms of former President Cardenas of Mexico, President Quezon took it upon himself to popularize this pro-labor policy. No sooner had he returned from his trip to the United States and Mexico in 1937 than he sounded the keynote of his program as follows: "It is my ambition that the Philippines shall become a country where poverty is unknown, where justice is the watchword, and democracy and freedom the motto."[3]

President Quezon took every opportunity to acquaint his countrymen with this policy. He reiterated it energetically on public occasions. The philosophy of social justice permeated almost all public measures. Early in 1938, in his annual message to the National Assembly, President Quezon paid a tribute to labor and appealed to the nation for immediate action in behalf of the working people. He said:

We are earnestly concerned with social justice. Without a strict application of social justice to all elements of the community, general satisfaction of the people with their government is impossible to achieve. Here, in the just and equitable solution of social problems, is the real test of the efficiency of democracy to meet present-day conditions of society. Social justice involves many and varied questions, such as taxation, wages, land ownership, insurance against accidents, old age, etc. . . . . almost alone the masses have built the Commonwealth by their sacrifices . . . . Now we are fully prepared to act, and we must act at once if our people are to continue placing their confidence for the remedy of the social evils which embitter their life entirely in our hands.[4]

Revolutionary in effect was the following statement of President Quezon regarding the relative importance of property rights and human rights:

The right of property in my opinion is essential only as a supplement to the right to live, and therefore is only secondary to

---

[3] *Manila Bulletin*, August 20, 1937.   [4] *Ibid.*, June 25, 1938.

that greater and more important right. . . . . I do believe in recognizing human rights in preference to property rights when there is a conflict. . . . . But when people accumulate wealth at the expense of the comforts of the rest of the population, I do not believe in that.[5]

The Social Justice program of the Commonwealth Government was much more than a mere statement of public policy relative to economic and particularly labor problems. It was a definite program for action. Its primary and immediate aim was to improve the conditions of the laboring class, but its fundamental and long-run objective loomed large in the background—that of laying a basis for a happy, prosperous, independent Philippines. Like all programs of reform, the Social Justice program can best be evaluated in the light of its accomplishments.

Apart from its general effect upon the country's economic progress, the program did a great deal for the laboring class. Just to mention a few positive measures: a Collective Bargaining Law and an Eight-hour Labor Law were passed; National Commissions of Labor and of Peasants were created under government sponsorship for labor unity; a National Social Security Administration was established for the unemployed; a Court of Industrial Relations was created for the arbitration of labor disputes; an Agricultural and Industrial Bank was created to facilitate "easy" credit for farmers and merchants with small capital; a National Resettlement Project Administration was established for the relief of the landless. The effectiveness of these institutional measures may be questioned, but the sincerity of the motive behind each can scarcely be doubted.

With all its theoretical weaknesses and practical limitations, the Social Justice program had a progressive effect on the national economy in general and on the labor movement in particular. It helped to curb excessive exploitation, for it was a constant reminder of "the social purpose and

[5] *Ibid.*, February 15, 1938.

duties of property." It moderated the conflict between capital and labor, in that it provided the machinery of collective bargaining. It promoted the material welfare of the laboring masses, placing special emphasis on the need for ameliorating their condition. It stimulated and encouraged the growth of labor organization in that it recognized the right of labor to organize. It exerted a liberalizing influence upon conservative employers, for it promised "a reasonable profit" in return for fulfilling their "obligations to labor and society." Finally, it promoted the utilitarian principle of the greatest good of the greatest number by recognizing the priority of human rights over property rights. In short, the program had the tendency to promote industrial peace and economic democracy.

How did the Filipino people react to the Social Justice program? The reaction of capital to the program was typified by the following criticism made by Judge Sumulong, a big landowner and the brain of the political opposition:

The so-called social justice program may now be judged by its fruits. It has been imported from the United States during this transition period, during the period of economic difficulties, when it was clearly inopportune to undertake any sort of experiment. It has produced intranquility and fear among our capitalists, thus aggravating through the diminution of enterprises and investments the already precarious situation of our laboring class. Before the inauguration of the Commonwealth, the difficulties between landowners and tenants could have been solved with the adoption of measures of simple justice without any necessity of arousing class hatred and antagonism which are now fast drawing our working class toward communism . . . . in a country like ours in which natural resources abound without being exploited and in which the industries are still in their infancy, although it is convenient to adopt preventive measures against the abuse of capitalism, it is an unpardonable imprudence to incite the working class to make extreme demands, discouraging in this way persons of initiative and organizations with means to help effectively in the material progress of the country.[6]

[6] *Manila Bulletin*, June 8, 1940.

Philippine business cried aloud against the Social Justice program and tried to discredit it by stigmatizing it as "communistic," much as American business went after the New Deal policy of the Roosevelt administration. On the other hand, labor voiced different objections to the program. For instance, the Socialist leader and supreme head of the General Workers' Union, Pedro Abad Santos, said:

The only way President Quezon can show his earnestness to carry into effect his so-called social justice program is to give his whole-hearted support to the labor movement, to make capital realize its obligations to labor and society. He cannot do it himself alone, for he is subject to constant pressure by powerful capitalist interest. The best support he can give the labor movement is not to call constabulary soldiers when there is a strike.[7]

The Communists likewise adopted a cautious attitude toward the program. Guillermo Capadocia, General Secretary of the Communist party and Executive Secretary of the presidium of the Collective Labor Movement, expressed this attitude as follows:

While we Communists keenly appreciate the progressive role of President Quezon in Philippine national life and do not cast any doubt as to the motives of his actions in the contingency of any future conflict between labor and capital, and while we Communists are always ready to aggressively support him in pushing his program of social justice, we cannot feel that we can call ourselves the vanguard of the working class movement if we did not warn the masses to be more vigilant and more alert in the protection and defense of their rights already acquired, against the onslaught of those reactionaries who will misinterpret President Quezon's fine motives for the people.[8]

The practical difficulties of the Social Justice program were caused not so much by capital or labor opposition as by its own inconsistencies. Hence the contradiction between theory and practice. President Quezon said that "social

[7] Convocation address at the College of Business Administration, University of the Philippines, Manila, February 1, 1940.

[8] G. Capadocia, "Strike—The Workers' Only Weapon," *The Vanguard*, Manila, March 1939.

justice can only mean justice to each and every social group," and "so long as capital is not unmindful of the social purpose and duties of property, so long will our government give it whole-hearted support and protection."[9] To do "every social group" justice is of course rhetorical, the idea being *ipso facto* impracticable under the existing economic arrangements. There is the rub. In the practical application of social justice the government is often forced to make its choice between the interests of capital and those of labor. It is open to question if the capitalist class can consistently attend to "the social purpose and duties of property" and reap "a reasonable profit."

While recognizing the primacy of human rights, President Quezon was quite uncompromising in his readiness to suppress anything and anybody that endangered property rights; he said: "Indeed it is my inescapable duty to protect property rights, and I shall use all the powers of the government in the discharge of this duty."[10] Strikes, picketing, and other trespasses on private property instantly provoked government action, even when these trespasses were actuated by the defense of human rights. Property rights were still considered "sacred," so sacred that the rights of persons were often sacrificed on their altar. For instance, in the province of Pampanga, Socialist tenants or workers were murdered in cold blood by private guards of sugar centrals or by the police—in the name of "peace and order." In an attempt to accord both capital and labor equal protection and just treatment, the government frequently satisfied one party at the expense of the other. To reconcile conflicting economic interests is a ticklish problem, the adequate solution of which would require a program much more drastic than a program of palliative measures.

[9] *Manila Bulletin*, February 16, 1938.
[10] *Ibid.*, March 13, 1939.

III

OBJECTIVES OF INDUSTRIALIZATION

In most Western countries, industrialization started with the triumph of capitalism over feudalism in general and as a logical consequence of the Industrial Revolution in particular. But in the Philippines industrialization was superimposed on a traditional agrarian economy. After the establishment of duty-free trade relations between the United States and the Philippines there developed a gradual concentration of industry around the agricultural export crops.

As such, the process of industrialization was narrow and unplanned. No one seemed to care much or to think seriously about industrializing the country; everybody seemed to think that the Philippines were somehow preordained to remain an agricultural country. Perhaps centuries of foreign domination accounted for this pessimistic outlook. Superficial industrialization, nevertheless, went on under the direct stimulus of a favorable American market.

Industrialization as a systematic Philippine program is a recent development. It began to assume a deliberate character when the Tydings-McDuffie Act was passed by the American Congress in 1934. Realization of possible economic dislocations incident to the loss of a favorable American market after the attainment of independence, scheduled for 1946, prompted a long-range program of industrialization. Facing the alternatives of risky competition in the world market and much-increased manufacture for domestic consumption, the Philippines chose the latter.

The intense economic nationalism that swept the entire world during the Great Depression was accentuated by the outbreak of World War II in September 1939. This strong shift toward economic nationalism came as an attempt on the part of nations to restore economic equilibrium and to isolate themselves from adverse economic and political con-

ditions in other countries. Every nation tried to get out of
the economic impasse at the expense of other nations.
Strong national feelings, a frantic armaments race, and
wars of aggression marked the new national and international adjustments.

Had it not been for preferential trade relations with
the United States, the Philippines might have suffered
severely from the ravages of neo-mercantilism. Yet these
preferential relations were scheduled to come to an end
sooner or later as political independence was realized, and
this gloomy prospect actuated a serious consideration of
industrialization for domestic consumption in the Philippines. Secretary of Finance Manuel Roxas explained the
Philippine response to international economic stimuli as
follows:

> The only workable economy possible under present condi-
> tions is a nationalistic economy on a producer-consumer basis.
> Every nation has adopted it to a greater or lesser degree . . . .
> Not being able to engage in a free interchange of production
> with other countries, we must endeavor to supply as much of our
> requirements as practicable with our own production. Self-
> sufficiency cannot be absolute, but it can be approximated, espe-
> cially in prime essentials.[1]

Thus Philippine industrialization was part and parcel
of the international drive toward national self-sufficiency,
a transitionary adjustment to coming political independence. "Producer-consumer economy" is the theoretical
expression for such adjustment. But "producer-consumer
economy" as applied to the Philippines had more fundamental goals than merely that of escaping the adverse
effects of losing a favorable American market. For, as
Secretary Roxas explained on the same occasion:

> There can only be one sound and just economy for the
> Philippines . . . . It is an economy that should safeguard the
> welfare of the masses, raising the standards of living of the whole

[1] Speech at the Ateneo de Manila, February 1939.

people rather than merely enhancing the wealth of a privileged class.

Secretary Roxas also proposed the democratic control of the means of production through co-operatives. He said:

> With increased production there will be needed numerous services for distribution and other facilities indispensable to a broader and more diversified economy. Many of these undertakings may be effected through co-operative associations which should place in the hands of the workers themselves the instruments of production and the power that goes with them.

He dispelled the impression that he favored radical socialism, by adding:

> The economy I am advocating has the added advantage that the control of production would be in the hands of a large portion of our people and not concentrated in a few wealthy groups—an economy based largely on a multitude of small independent farms and workshops, insuring a wider distribution of the fruits of industry.

This looks like a version of Guild Socialism and raises the same questions: How can "a multitude of small independent farms and workshops" compete effectively with gigantic, well-organized trusts, corporations, and other monopolies? How can the control of production be shifted from the hands of "a few wealthy groups" to those of "a large portion of our people"? The burden of proof lies with those who propose such a system.

By way of criticizing the opponents of his "producer-consumer economy," Secretary Roxas said in the same speech:

> To say that unless preferential trade with the United States were indefinitely extended our situation would be utterly hopeless is to adopt a defeatist attitude which is neither justified nor in keeping with our political aspirations . . . . It is well to insist that preferential trade be extended sufficiently long to permit an orderly adjustment of our economy, but for anyone to say that the only solution for our economic problems now and when we shall be free is perpetuation of preferential trade is in itself a renuncia-

tion of independence . . . . After we have adjusted our economy,
and provided we produce more and develop the home market,
preferential trade should not be essential to the Philippines. If
we can find foreign markets for our products let us profit by those
markets. But whether we have new markets or not, let us produce
to supply as much of our domestic requirements as practicable.
Such a policy would not only insure for us a more stable economy
during the period of adjustment, but would make possible the
strengthening of our economic position and the maintenance and
improvement of our social standards after independence and after
abrogation of existing trade preferences.

The Filipino beneficiaries of a favorable American
market pinned their hopes on the possibility of the indefinite
extension of preferential trade with the United States. They
therefore favored the establishment in the Philippines of
an American dominion or protectorate, or a permanent
Commonwealth status under American protection. Typical,
for example, is the following appeal that appeared in a
Manila periodical allegedly subsidized by the sugar interests:

It does not matter what kind of person you are, whether rich
or poor, mighty or weak. But it does matter a lot, however, for
you to contribute your share in the gigantic task of preserving the
independence of our beloved country so that our children coming
after us will enjoy its full benefits. Help us apprise the Filipino
people that the continued political relations between America and
the Philippines is our best guarantee. This is not much to ask
of you.[2]

The controversy between "producer-consumer economy" and preferential trade remained undecided. Loss of
the favorable American market seemed almost inevitable
before the Pacific War broke out. The Philippines had as
yet experienced less than one year's application of declining quotas and of increasing export taxes on the six
restricted-export products: cordage, coconut oil, buttons,
sugar, cigars, and leaf tobacco. The trade statistics made

[2] "Invitation to Patriotism," *The Commonwealth Advocate*, August 1940.

the situation look worse than it actually was. With the increased importance of gold and base minerals among the exports, the relative proportion of sugar, coconut oil, and other export crops in the total had become so small as to make these branches look like "declining industries"; but the decline was only relative.

Even this, however, had the effect of discouraging further capital investments in the production of the major-export crops. Many investors took it for granted that in the future external trade would more and more be pushed into the background and production for domestic consumption would correspondingly come to the fore. Yet even a large program of industrialization for the manufacture of consumer goods need not stand in the way of a sizable foreign trade. Especially, until the country can produce more of its own "prime essentials," it will have to import both consumer and producer goods which can be paid for only by a continued large-scale exportation of raw materials.

The elimination of foreign trade except with Japan during the Japanese occupation—if such it can be called—should not materially change the basic trend toward increased production for the home market; for Japan, even with wartime needs, can hardly replace the United States either as a market for Philippine products or as an exporter of finished goods required by the Philippines. If economic nationalism is replaced by more or less free international trade, including capital movements, then the Philippines will be able to enjoy the fruits of freer trade relations with other nations. In such an event, industrialization for the home market will not be essential.

Whether or not the Philippines should produce for the world market in competition with other countries more highly industrialized is a moot question. E. D. Hester, long associated with the Philippine government and now Economic Adviser to the United States High Commissioner to the Philippines, not long ago expressed the belief that

the type of industrial organization desirable for the Philippines in the future is that "which, making the most use
of the unfinished materials found within the community,
manufactures finished goods mainly for consumption by
the community itself."[3] However, there is no reason why
the Philippines should not produce for world consumption
those products which it can produce advantageously, that
is, mainly tropical products.

In outlining the economic objectives of the Philippines,
Secretary of Agriculture and Commerce Benigno S. Aquino
listed the following agencies, policies, and problems of
industrialization:

> Government agencies and policies: (1) Creation of a National
> Economic Council to plan the national economy preparatory to
> independence. (2) Organization of the National Research Coun-
> cil for technical and organized research. (3) Execution by the
> National Development Company of findings and recommendations
> of the above Councils. (4) Experimental enterprises and studies
> by the Department of Agriculture and Commerce and its subordi-
> nate agencies along industrialization. (5) Preferential purchases
> by government of local products. (6) The Abaca Advisory Com-
> mittee. (7) The Tobacco Board. (8) The Economic Conference
> Commission.
>
> Some problems: (1) Determination of replacing such im-
> ported products by local production as may be advantageously
> produced. (2) Determination of rationalizing the production of
> such Philippine exports as may meet world competition.[4]

In this connection it may be interesting to compare the
following order of industries suggested by Miss Mary Van
Kleeck, of the Russell Sage Foundation, for consideration
in planning the productive basis for higher standards of
living:

1. Iron and steel
2. Machinery and the metal trades, including the key industry of
   making the machines which make machines

[3] "Footnotes to Philippine Economics," *The Philippine Social Science
Review*, May 1940.
[4] "Philippine Economic Objectives," *Business*, Manila, November 1938.

3. Food production, including both agricultural and processing
4. Power
5. Construction of all forms of shelter, including production of
   building materials as well as the actual process of building
6. Clothing, with the textile industry as its center
7. Industries of organic chemistry and other types of process
   industries[5]   589789

Since the avowed purpose of Philippine industrialization is "raising the standards of living of the whole people," such a "productive basis" as suggested by Miss Van Kleeck is worth serious study. However, the order of industries cited above cannot be applied to the Philippines mechanically. Countries like the United States and the Soviet Union can build heavy industry advantageously in order later to enjoy a higher standard of consumption. But a country like the Philippines is economically better suited for light industry. The development of heavy industry or capital-goods industries in the Philippines is expedient if, for economic or political reasons, the country cannot import or does not desire to import capital goods from abroad. But as long as other countries produce capital goods more economically and as long as the Philippines have the ability to import them, there is no good reason why the Philippines should develop capital-goods industries. Barring autarchy or war, the Philippines will be able to raise its standard of consumption through a combination of foreign trade and domestic light industry. Secretary of Finance Roxas expressed a similar view when he said:

It may be asked, what shall we buy from abroad if we are to produce all our requirements at home? My reply is that we would buy those articles which grow in number and in variety with the advancement of our culture and wealth. We shall buy machinery, chemicals, automobiles, airplanes, armaments, and many other commodities which we could not produce economically. To that extent at least we need to sell abroad.[6]

[5] Mary Van Kleeck, *et al., On Economic Planning* (Covici-Friede, New York, 1935).

[6] Manuel Roxas' Ateneo de Manila speech, February 1939.

In line with Secretary Roxas' "producer-consumer economy," the Philippines had made a good start in the development of light and consumer-goods industries. The government-owned National Development Company began operating textile, cement, and canning factories and cotton plantations. The Bureau of Plant Industry promoted cotton culture. The Bureau of Commerce, in co-operation with the Bureau of Plant Industry, promoted home weaving. The Bureau of Science started its experiments on building materials for roofing and on new food and clothing materials. Many other measures of industrialization were either put into effect or were under consideration.[7] The industrialization movement in the Philippines would have made great strides had it not been for the sudden outbreak of the war in the Pacific.

In discussing the problem of Philippine industrialization, Miss Catherine Porter observes:

> If the country cannot sell its sugar, why not sell some of its other agricultural produce? If it cannot sell enough to pay for purchases abroad, why not produce more of those goods at home? If agriculture no longer pays, why not industrialize? The answer is that these things must be done, but they take time and money and intelligent planning.[8]

The Philippines will doubtless utilize the lessons to be drawn from a rich international experience in economic planning. So long as Philippine industrialization stays in line with its aim of "raising the standards of living of the whole people," it will be dynamic, progressive, and expansive. But the minute it deviates from this aim, it will become static, conservative, and restrictive. It takes the collective will and action of all the people involved in the fulfillment of the industrialization program to avoid this danger.

[7] See Secretary Aquino's article, *loc. cit.*

[8] *Far Eastern Survey*, June 29, 1938.

IV

CONDITIONS OF LABOR

Levels of Living

Owing to the American influence, the Philippines had the highest "standard of living" (except real income)[1] in the Far East, with the possible exception of Japan. Yet its actual plane of living (existing real income) stood below its standard of living and was, before the war, lower than that of some other Oriental countries. Judging, not from the Western standard of living, but from an objective standard necessary for the well-being of any human being, the Filipino working class live far below the absolute minimum standard of "health and efficiency."

The low plane of living is indicated by the low per capita income of the country. In 1939, Secretary of Finance Manuel Roxas estimated the annual per capita income of the Philippines at ₱80, i.e., $40.[2] While per capita income hides the inequality of income distribution and fails to register the degree of real satisfaction derived from actual consumption, it is a good index of national welfare, efficiency, and productivity. If the national income were equally distributed, an average income of ₱80 a year would place every man, woman, and child in the Philippines at a few points above the subsistence level, inasmuch as the average per capita cost of bare subsistence amounts to ₱75 a year. If the cost of living were to rise even only a little faster than income, the majority of the Filipino workers would find themselves at the level of "primary poverty."

According to a survey of financial status of families in some districts of Manila, made by the Department of Health in 1940, over 30,000 working families were living on that

[1] A standard of living may be defined as goods and services needed to satisfy the prevalent notion of an adequate living.

[2] Manuel Roxas' Ateneo de Manila speech.

37

"poverty level," 4,541 families on the "health and efficiency level," and only 909 families on the "comfort level."[3] This is by no means an isolated example, for another investigator[4] found that in Occidental Negros, out of 120 families investigated, some earned only ₱60 during the entire year and made an average yearly income of ₱34. Allowing for other income than money incomes and for the lower cost of living in the provinces, rural working families enjoyed no higher plane of living than urban working families. Even if the national income of one billion pesos[5] were doubled, labor incomes would not be raised correspondingly under the existing system of distribution.

It is probable that the actual consumption level of the Filipino *people as a whole* rose greatly owing to free and preferential trade with the United States. However, the popular belief that the Filipino *working class* enjoyed a higher level of living under the American regime than under the Spanish regime does not square with facts and figures. No less a person than President Quezon dispelled that popular impression when he said in an annual message to the National Assembly:

The men and women who till the soil or work in the factories are hardly better off now than they were during the Spanish regime. Of course, wages have increased as compared with those paid when we were under the sovereignty of Spain, and these wages are higher than in any other Oriental country, with the possible exception of Japan. But it should be remembered that money could buy more in those Spanish days than it can now, and furthermore, in the relationship between employer and employee in the days of old, there was a consideration of higher value to the employee than the monetary compensation itself.[6]

[3] *Journal of the Philippine Medical Association*, November 1940, p. 690.

[4] I. T. Runes, *General Standards of Living and Wages of Workers in the Philippine Sugar Industry* (Philippine Council, Institute of Pacific Relations, Manila, 1939).

[5] Manuel Roxas, *loc. cit.*

[6] *Labor Bulletin*, September 1939.

Shredding hemp to form "slivers"

Sorting best-quality hemp on the Ohta Plantation, Davao

Higher nominal incomes give the illusion of a higher plane of living, but this illusion disappears in the face of the high cost of living. President Quezon's assertion that money income has increased is true as far as the wage scales of the Spanish and the American regimes are concerned. But since the American occupation the price level has gone far ahead of the wage level. Until 1929, the peak year of all time and the beginning of the Great Depression, nominal incomes continued to go upward steadily. In 1929, Professor Velmonte, of the College of Agriculture, University of the Philippines, and the Bureau of Labor estimated money incomes of workers and peasants at between ₱500 and ₱600 a year.[7] After 1929, money incomes and costs of living both declined, the former probably more rapidly. According to a survey made in 1940 by the *Manila Bulletin,* the average annual money income of all factory workers in the Philippines amounted to ₱240 and that of all agricultural families to ₱200.[8] Thus, from 1929 to 1940, money incomes declined by more than 50 per cent.

However, nominal income *per se* fails to indicate the material well-being of the working class. It is *real* income that counts. The real incomes of the Filipino working class declined even more sharply than their money incomes, because of a steady increase in the cost of living. The number of the average Filipino working family being five, the per capita labor income amounted to somewhere around ₱50 a year, which is considerably less than the ₱80 per capital national income. Viewed from the standpoint of actual consumption or real income, the Filipino working class experienced less and less satisfaction in the post-depression period.[9]

[7] I. P. Runes, *op. cit.*

[8] Compiled from figures of daily wages, *Manila Bulletin,* February 26, 1940.

[9] This statement takes household budgets as the basis for appraisals of the level of living. In the Philippines, the decline in the levels of living during the depression period was mitigated more than in other tropical

Clemente takes the extreme view that the American regime has had no beneficial effect on Filipino levels of living:

The bare truth of the matter is that the prosperity which American imperialism is supposed to have brought to the Philippines has affected only one per cent of our population. The huge exports of sugar and other products to the United States, while they are made mostly by Philippine labor, leave only subsistence incomes to the workers. The beneficiaries of the preference in the American market are not Filipino citizens. They are Americans, Spaniards, and other foreigners. A few Filipinos, so-called, also participate, but these are usually Spaniards who only recently took out Filipino citizenship.[10]

This unfavorable reflection on the American regime as well as on the Philippine economy fails to consider that the population might have been much worse off had it not been for preferential trade with the United States. In his convocation speech at the College of Business Administration, University of the Philippines, on February 1, 1940, Pedro Abad Santos also mentioned the declining level of living of the Filipino masses:

As it is now, we, the workers, are shouldering all the burden of the economic depression and our living standard is going from bad to worse, while the *propietarios, hacenderos* and capitalists enjoy themselves in luxury. The poor get poorer and the rich richer.

Whatever may be the basis for this assertion, the growth of city conveniences and a rising plane of living among the well-to-do created the illusion of an improvement in conditions which certainly was not widespread.[11] Sometimes

countries by an unusually well-developed system of public services—supported not from taxes on individual earnings but from taxes on the special profits made possible by free trade with the United States and by the Philippines' favorable position in balance of international payments.

[10] C. Clemente, "The Economic Conditions of the Philippines—1938," *Kalayan*, Manila, July 15, 1939.

[11] The Filipino sociologist, Serafin E. Macaraig, in one of his textbooks points to the precariousness of the high planes of living that have evolved in the Filipino middle class without an adequate economic foundation (*Social Problems*, Manila, 1929, p. 273 *et al.*).

when unrest was rife in a group of workers, they would
be reminded that, with all their lack of material comforts,
they were better off than the masses in China, Netherlands
India, and other Oriental countries. But even the relatively large number of automobiles in use and the relatively
high money wages earned in some occupations did not
appease those who compared the poverty of the masses with
the seeming affluence of limited circles. In this regard,
E. D. Hester made the following observation:

> The Philippines is a high-wage area in the midst of the world's
> most notable low-wage area. By this I mean that every one of our
> neighbors pays lower wages for a day's factory labor than we do.
> Behind a wall of tariff protection, we have adopted standards of
> living in matters other than the common dietary which are higher
> and require higher wages than is the case in the East Indies,
> China, or Japan. Much of our high wage level is artificial because
> also we have high food and clothing costs for the plain people,
> so that real wages—purchasing power—are not as high as the
> wage rates expressed in pesos would indicate.[12]

Wages in Industry

Americanization of the Philippines had not progressed
to the extent of introducing the American wage scale into
the native economy. The low wage level in the Philippines
was the result of colonial conditions which permitted neither
a rapid progress in productivity nor the growth of a strong
trade-union movement.

In 1938 the Department of Labor made a survey of
wage levels in 619 industrial and commercial firms
throughout the Islands. Out of 107,923 workers covered
by the survey, 33,045, or 30.62 per cent, received daily
wages of under ₱1.00; and 7,932, or 7.35 per cent, earned
daily wages of over ₱2.40.[13] This was the wage situation,
not in small enterprises, but in such large and profitable
industries as mines, sugar centrals, lumber sawmills, coco-
nut-drying factories, shoe factories, railroads, bus-trans-

---

[12] E. D. Hester, *loc. cit.*   [13] *Labor Bulletin*, September 1939.

portation companies, electric-power plants, and cigar and cigarette factories. In 1939 the Department of Labor estimated the average daily wage of Filipino workers at ₱.90.[14] In 1940 the *Manila Bulletin* survey already quoted disclosed that the daily wage paid by factories all over the country averaged ₱.80. With the preponderance of small-scale enterprises, the majority of the Filipino industrial workers were living on a monthly wage of less than ₱30. The wage situation evoked the following official comment:

> It is true, industrial development has widened opportunities for employment, and fairly good wages are paid for skilled occupations; but the wages of the great bulk of common laborers in industry are merely enough for bare existence. It is in the industrial field where alarm has been caused of late by the widespread strikes and threats of strikes.[15]

Measured in terms of money, labor costs in the Philippines, before the war, were a little lower than in Japan and much lower than in the United States. But, measured in terms of effort or sacrifice, Philippine labor was more expensive than either American or Japanese labor. In America high productivity offsets high wages; hence unit costs are low. In Japan high-productive efficiency before the war was confined to a few industries, such as textile, munitions, shipping, and some export industries. Both China and the Philippines have low wages; yet they are high-cost countries except in lines of production which require much hand labor, such as laces, carved wood, embroideries, and shell-craft. That is why many of the Philippine products cannot compete in the world market.

Commonwealth Act No. 37, as amended by Executive Order No. 105, fixed the minimum wage for common laborers in government employment at ₱1.25 for Manila and ₱1.00 for the provinces. However, less than half of the provinces were found in 1940 to be paying the legal mini-

---

[14] *Labor Bulletin*, September 1939.
[15] *Manila Bulletin*, February 26, 1940.

mum wage of ₱1.00 to their public-works laborers.[16] In 1939 only one native firm in Manila, the Elizalde Paint and Rope Factory, and very few American firms in the capital, maintained the minimum wage of ₱1.00 or more. Before the war there was no minimum wage law in the Philippines applicable to all private firms. The adoption of the minimum wage by private concerns was a voluntary matter. However, in 1940 practically all the transportation companies were reported as paying more than a minimum daily wage of ₱1.00.[17] According to J. H. Marsman, Netherlands mining executive in Manila, "the mining industry adopted a peso-a-day wage scale long before the government established that figure as a required basic wage."[18] This was true of some of the sugar mills also.

Judge Francisco Zulueta, of the Court of Industrial Relations, created a sensation among businessmen as well as workers when he ruled that "wages, decent wages at that, should constitute a lien on business, and should not be made to depend on the profits or losses of the employer."[19] This ruling must have disappointed also those professional economists who have dogmatic faith in the "marginal-productivity theory" of wages; for Judge Zulueta was in effect going against the orthodox idea of paying no more or no less than the equivalent of the value (to the employer) of the product of the marginal (additional) unit of labor hired. In other words, Judge Zulueta, though not an economist, must have felt that the orthodox principle of maximizing profits was inconsistent with the Social Justice program of the government.

The general backwardness of industry, perpetuated as it was by colonial conditions, kept down the productivity of labor and hence the wage level. The low scale of living of the peasantry dragged down the wage level of the industrial workers, and the low productivity of handicraft

---

[16] *Ibid.*   [17] *Ibid.*

[18] *Manila Bulletin,* October 4, 1940.   [19] *Ibid.,* September 7, 1938.

industry kept down the wages of the factory workers. Furthermore, a large population in proportion to available capital in the pre-depression years, increasing unemployment in the 1930's, lack of social insurance, weak trade-unionism, predominance of small-scale enterprises, absence of a nation-wide minimum-wage law—all these and other factors accounted for low wage levels in Philippine industry. The Department of Labor gave this official view of the social implications of the wage situation:

> There can be no economic stability among the masses as long as the wages at present received by our laborers continue to be meager; nor is it possible for a housewife to make miracles with a ninety-centavo daily income . . . . The inevitable result is the slums, malnutrition, lack of medical attendance, and heavy infant mortality, and children out of school trying to undersell labor in competition with adults.[20]

As the bargaining strength of organized labor grows *pari passu* with industrialization, the wage level of Philippine industry will undoubtedly become higher. The workers' struggle for higher wages is as natural as it is inevitable.

Wages in Agriculture

Ninety-two per cent of all landholders owned from one hectare to less than five. They were not, therefore, "farmers" as Americans know them; they had in income the status of the poorest type of sharecropper. Together with tenants and farm hands, they constituted the peasantry of the Philippines. It is, therefore, necessary to consider the income status of tenants as well as the wage level of agricultural laborers.

The daily wages of agricultural laborers in 1939 ran from a minimum of ₱.15 to a maximum of ₱2.00 throughout the Islands, or an average minimum of ₱.42 and an average maximum of ₱1.05.[21] The Bureau of the Census

---

[20] *Labor Bulletin*, September 1939.   [21] *Ibid.*, May 1939.

in 1941 gave the following statistical data on the wage situation in Pampanga, one of the most prosperous provinces and "the hotbed of radicalism": 652 agriculturists, including 100 farm laborers, were making less than ₱.10 a day; 2,358 were receiving a wage of from ₱.10 to ₱.19 a day; 3,292 reported wages of ₱.20 to ₱.29 a day.[22] The 1940 *Manila Bulletin* survey revealed that the average farm hand is paid ₱.50 a day.[23] Thus agricultural workers received lower average wages than industrial workers, whose average rate was thirty centavos more, i.e., ₱.80 a day. This discrepancy between industrial and agricultural wage rates, as all over the world, is a reflection partly of the lower productivity of labor in the fields but also of less-developed labor organization. In general, agricultural laborers in all provinces, including the rich sugar areas, were reported as receiving "starvation wages."[24]

In spite of commercial money crops which found their way into the American market, the masses of landless laborers remained in extreme poverty. A wealthy sugar planter admitted the unwholesome situation that obtained in the sugar fields as follows:

While our enormous profits have resulted in the acquisition of luxuries which the wealthy consider necessary, our laborers have continued to live in shacks in penury. Year after year, poverty from which they feel there is no escape has been their common, unchanging lot. When the laborer is paid such starvation wages as 30 or 40 centavos a day, is it any wonder that the seeds of discontent should sprout in the sugar fields with alarming rapidity, sprinkled as they are in secret with the water of agitation and class hatred and tilled with the tools of propaganda?[25]

After his investigation in the sugar-growing regions, I. T. Runes reached a similar conclusion:

[22] *Manila Bulletin*, July 23, 1941.   [23] *Ibid.*, February 26, 1940.

[24] *Ibid.*, November 15, 1938.

[25] Ramon Lopez, "To My Fellow Hacenderos," *The National Review*, Manila, April 23, 1937.

Because of sugar, Occidental Negros and Pampanga stand as the richest provinces in the Philippines, and their people as the most prosperous. But, undoubtedly, because of sugar that has sweetened the life of a few thousand planters and mill owners, about two million people in the sugar areas of the country live the most miserable and deplorable existence, in comparison with those in regions where other agricultural crops are raised. So deplorable is their condition that labor troubles center around plantations where wages of landless laborers are not only apparently but also obviously inadequate to cover living expenses.[26]

If such was the wage situation in the prosperous sugar areas, it would be reasonable to infer that the situation was even worse in the less prosperous areas. However, this was not the case, for, as the Lava study[27] of the rice-growing Ilocos region showed, agricultural laborers in other than sugar areas were comparatively better paid. In other words, agricultural laborers producing big-money crops were subjected to greater exploitation than those producing staples like rice.

Rosendo Regalada, chief of the Division of Labor Statistics of the Department of Labor, gives a good summary of the whole wage situation in Philippine agriculture as follows:

Our exports of staple products have increased by leaps and bounds, and yet the wages of our agricultural laborers, averaging sixty centavos a day, have practically remained where they were two decades ago. Inasmuch as this class covers about 80 per cent of our labor population, our much vaunted prosperity has not even touched the toiling masses of the soil.[28]

The 1936 Fact-Finding Survey of the government estimated that 10,500 tenants, working an average of two hectares each in a total area of 41,600 hectares in the rice-growing regions of Central and Southern Luzon, were

---

[26] Runes, *op. cit.*

[27] Horacio Lava, *Levels of Living in the Ilocos Region*, Philippine Council, Institute of Pacific Relations, Manila, 1938.

[28] *Labor Bulletin*, September 1939.

receiving an average annual income of ₱122 per family. That is to say, those tenants were earning, in effect, an average daily wage of ₱.36, which is less than either the *Manila Bulletin* figure of ₱.50 or the Department of Labor figure of ₱.60 for agricultural laborers. Thus the tenants were no better off than "farm hands." However, this same government survey found that 26 per cent of the tenant families investigated were earning a total annual net income of ₱250.[29]

Later figures of "farm income" show better financial standing for tenants than for agricultural laborers. The Lava study of Ilocos tenant families placed their average annual income at ₱257.59, while the Runes survey of southern sugar workers estimated their average annual income at ₱184.86. One writer pictured the economic status of the tenant farmers in the neighborhood of a typical "Philippine Middletown" as follows:

> In general, the standard of living is extremely low . . . . What makes existence possible for these people and the tenant farmers around here is the fact that they all have more or less rice and make out on this with an occasional frog, mudfish, or some fruit. Practically all of them are in debt and disheartened. It is hard to understand how they manage to be so law-abiding.[30]

As far as the low incomes of tenant farmers were concerned, over-manning and under-capitalization and hence the operation of the law of diminishing returns were the underlying causes. However, the law of diminishing returns operated not only on those under-capitalized farms but also on large farms where improvements in the means

[29] The figures here cited and others cited below do not, of course, represent the total income of farm families. One survey, for example, revealed that two-fifths of the labor time of a group of 740 tenants was devoted to secondary occupations, 28 per cent of their income was derived from secondary occupations, and 12 per cent of it from household industries. (Hester, Mabbun, *et al.*, "Some Economic and Social Aspects of Philippine Rice Tenancies," *Philippine Agriculturist*, XII (1924), 9.)

[30] Anonymous, "A Philippine Middletown," *Philippine Magazine*, Manila, June 1939.

and methods of production did not keep pace with the increase in the number of laborers employed. With some 65 per cent of the labor population concentrated in agriculture on the limited area of arable land actually under cultivation, diminishing productivity was the inevitable tendency of Philippine agriculture as a whole. More scientific farming, growth of farmers' co-operatives, expansion of the cultivated area, and other measures would help to counteract this general tendency. But there was nothing in Philippine farming which promised higher incomes for tenant farmers.

One answer to the question of the low incomes of tenants is the replacement of tenant farming by the wage system—but not as long as the wage system retains the custom of payment in kind. Where tenants and farm hands were strongly organized, as in Pampanga and its neighboring provinces, there was hope that the wage level of agricultural labor would improve. It was anticipated that the farm income, and the income of agricultural labor with it, would be adversely affected by the gradual loss of the American market for such Philippine products as sugar and coconut oil. Protective tariffs and artificial scarcity would not help to raise the farm income in the long run. The most important thing therefore would be to raise the productive efficiency of Philippine agriculture in general and that of agricultural labor in particular.

V

CONDITIONS OF LABOR (Continued)

Hours of Work

American influence was more manifest in hours of work than in any other aspect of labor conditions in the Philippines; the country had, before 1942, the shortest working week in the Orient. Roughly, the average daily hours of work for China were eleven, for Japan ten, and for the Philippines nine. However, in all these countries agricultural workers worked longer.

In 1937 the majority of the workers worked eight hours, although in a number of industries, such as embroidery, shoemaking, cigar factories, and retail shops, nine and ten hours of labor were common. In other lines of employment, such as drug stores, hotels, and cafes, many of the employees worked more than twelve hours. That is to say, of the 994 firms inspected by the Department of Labor in that year, 60.99 per cent maintained an eight-hour day for their workers. This is a fairly good record, considering the negligible enforcement of the eight-hour labor law of 1933.

A new eight-hour labor law was passed on June 3, 1939, after much controversy among labor leaders, businessmen, and government authorities. The following were the pertinent features of the new law (Commonwealth Act No. 444): the coverage extended to all workers but agricultural laborers, piece workers, domestic servants, and members of the family of the employer working for him; overtime work was to be compensated "at the same rate as their regular wages or salary, plus at least 25 per cent additional"; no employers, except public utilities, might compel an employee to work during Sundays and holidays without payment of an additional sum of at least 25 per cent of his regular wage; any violation of the Act was to be punished with a fine of not more than ₱1,000 or imprisonment for not more than one year, or both.

The coverage was not extensive enough, but even more important was the lack of provision against wage cuts incident to the shortening of working days. The new eight-hour law embodied such a provision in its original draft, but this was subsequently dropped under the protest of business "pressure groups." No comprehensive official data on working hours were made available after the enactment of the law, but there is reason to believe that in the lines of employment covered by the law the eight-hour day was at least more strictly observed than before 1939. However, many cases involving the violation of the law were brought before the Department of Labor for settlement after its passage.

Accident and Sickness

Industrial accidents and injuries were attributable in the Philippines largely to supervisory causes and only to a much smaller extent to physical or mechanical causes. Popular discussions did not distinguish injuries from accidents; they were treated as if they meant one and the same thing. Yet the distinction is important from the standpoint of accident prevention and costs. Not all accidents result in injuries; but every accident has the potentiality of producing injury. Therefore it is necessary that every accident, whether or not it results in injuries, be investigated with a view to discovering its causes and to preventing its recurrence. Competent students of accident prevention agree that it is not only possible but practicable to effect at least a four-fifths reduction in present accident frequency and accident cost.[1] However, it is difficult to share such optimism regarding the immediate prospect of accident prevention in the Philippines. Theoretically, the levying of the costs of industrial injuries on the employers encourages them to adopt a sound policy of accident pre-

[1] Cf. Committee on Elimination of Waste in Industry of the Federated American Engineering Societies, *Waste in Industry*, New York, 1921.

vention. But in practice this was not the case in the Philippines. This point will receive further attention in connection with sickness.

From 1933 to 1937 the Department of Labor handled a total of 20,089 accident cases. Of this number 1,174 were reported as fatal.[2] The details showed that the number of accidents and injuries increased rather than decreased from year to year, especially that of "fatal cases." A partial explanation of this unfavorable development may lie in the increased number and operation of hazardous industries, especially mining. Of 5,175 accident cases reported during 1938, 1,656 occurred in the mining industry, 987 in the transportation and communication industries, 579 in the lumber and timber industry, and 1,143 in the manufacturing and mechanical industries.[3] With respect to fatality the order was: forestry, government projects, transportation and communications. More workers fell victims to permanent and temporary disabilities in the mining industry and in transportation and communications than in other lines. Yet these are the industries that can well afford safety devices and other preventive measures.

The Workmen's Compensation Act No. 3428, as amended by Act No. 3812 and Commonwealth Act No. 210, provided for death benefits and specific compensation for specific injuries but not according to loss of earning power as the Compensation Law of California does. The Philippine Compensation Law excluded injuries caused by "(1) the voluntary intent of the employee to inflict such injury upon himself or another person; (2) drunkenness on the part of the laborer who had the accident; (3) notorious negligence of the same." The last condition of disqualification is the relic of the old Employers' Liability Law, viz., the doctrine of "contributory negligence," and is a source of much confusion in contested cases. Both as a measure of accident prevention and as a measure of financial relief

[2] *Labor Bulletin*, August 1938.   [3] *Ibid.*, June 1939.

for the injured, the Philippine Compensation Law fell short of the minimum essentials. It did not *fully* live up to the purposes of workmen's compensation, i.e.: (1) prevention of industrial accidents and injuries; (2) provision of medical service; and (3) cash compensation. However, there was an increasing tendency to regard the industrial system as responsible for the safety and protection of workers.

Of the commonly recognized causes of sickness the following are particularly obvious in the Philippines: the general social environment, including deficient disease control, impure water (in the provinces), bad housing, and poor public sanitation; the general labor situation, including inadequate wages, undernourishment, and inadequate medical and nursing care.

Tuberculosis is known as "a poverty disease," for it is most prevalent among families of low income. Records[4] show that about a seventh of the total mortality in the Philippines is caused by tuberculosis and that approximately a third of all deaths from preventable diseases are attributable to that cause. Dr. S. A. Francisco, chief of the Tuberculosis Control Section of the Bureau of Health, revealed that of the total number of deaths between 1932 and 1936 pulmonary tuberculosis accounted for 13.3 per cent, beriberi 8.1 per cent, influenza 4.4, malaria 4.1, dysentery 2.3, and typhoid 0.5 per cent. Dr. Francisco reported the number of tuberculosis cases in 1936 as 32,329. The number increased to 46,715 in 1938, according to the *Annual Report* of the Bureau of Health.[5]

Formerly the educational, diagnostic, and curative aspects of the problem of tuberculosis control were emphasized; but later preventive work came to be considered paramount. Significantly enough, the national tuberculosis program of the Philippines included, under preventive work, "improvements of the general nutrition and standard

[4] *Journal of the Philippine Medical Association*, September 1938.
[5] For fiscal year ended December 31, 1938, p. 47.

of living of the masses." Indicative of growing awareness of the vital relationship between sickness and poverty also was the following editorial comment of the Philippine Medical Association:

> The greatest problem of the Philippine Commonwealth today, according to our leaders, is to insure economic stability for the country. The government has launched a vast economic program with the end in view of increasing production, thereby augmenting the per capita wealth of the people . . . . But economics and medical care are intimately linked together. If we have to readjust our major economic policy it becomes necessary to recast also our medical set-up . . . . We hereby respectfully suggest to the government authorities concerned the advisability of recommending to the President of the Commonwealth the appointment of a technical committee to study this great problem of medical care of our laborers and tenants. These people constitute the backbone of our country. The strength of our nation depends upon their individual health and welfare. The Philippines is an agricultural country—and will remain so for many years to come—and unless the health of the tenants, especially, is assiduously guarded, poverty will ever remain hovering in our midst, and our beautiful economic planning may not attain its paramount objectives: happiness and social security of our people.[6]

Commonwealth Act No. 445, approved June 3, 1939, compelled all establishments with more than 400 employees to maintain an infirmary or emergency hospital together with a stock of medicines and the services of a physician, except where a hospital existed in the locality, in which case the employers were required to make an arrangement with the hospital for the care of their injured or sick employees. In the absence of voluntary and compulsory health insurance, such a legislative provision for hospitalization of sick laborers is a matter of absolute necessity. "Socialized medicine" is badly needed in the Philippines, but the Philippine Medical Association, like the American Medical Association, seemed indifferent, if not hostile, to the idea. In view of this professional attitude,

[6] *Journal of the Philippine Medical Association*, September 1938.

the government had not gone very far toward compulsory health insurance.

Factory inspections were periodically conducted by the Department of Labor in order to enforce existing laws relative to the promotion of health and safety of the workers. In 1938, for example, the Department covered 3,974 firms employing 242,539 laborers. Junior Safety Engineer R. B. Beleno, of the Department, after an inspection tour in the Bicol provinces in July 1938, reported the following typical case:

> The emergency dispensary of the mining company at Lahuy Island, Caramoan, Camarines Sur, was found inadequately furnished, dirty and lacking in personnel. Administering to the medical needs of more than four hundred people is a single physician without any helper . . . . Generally, the sanitary and hygienic conditions of the firms were found to be far from satisfactory.

Not only insanitary and unsafe factory conditions but also the slum conditions in which workers and their families live have a good deal to do with industrial accidents and diseases. After a survey of the slums in and around Manila, Speaker Yulo of the National Assembly observed:

> The people whom I saw living in the slums were living worse than animals. The air was foul, and whatever small space was available as a sort of park was set aside for comfort stations around which children played, in the absence of a decent playground.[7]

An explanatory note to the 1940 housing bill explains the matter:

> It is not surprising that discontent is prevalent among the underprivileged for they cannot provide themselves with the necessary means of decent living. Tired, heavily burdened, and living in mosquito-infested slums, at rents which greatly reduce their small incomes, the poor laborers and low-salaried employees encounter a bitter struggle for existence. They are dissatisfied with life, and they become a menace to peace and order if their

[7] *Manila Bulletin*, February 2, 1940.

Girls in Balintowoc costume packing cigarettes in one of the
factories in Manila

Women working in a Manila cigar factory

problem is not solved . . . . To alleviate their sufferings, to
provide them with better housing facilities, and to carry out the
principles of social justice, the housing program of the government should be pushed through without further delay so as to
prevent agitators from spreading the seeds of Communism among
our workers and laborers.

Whether the motive of such a housing program is to
destroy Communist tendencies or to improve the living condition of the laboring masses, the fact remains that cheap
yet sanitary living quarters are sorely needed by many
laborers and their families and would contribute toward
the effective protection of the workers' health and efficiency.

By way of summary, it seems apropos to cite the following statement of Dr. José Santillan, medical inspector
of the Department of Labor, regarding the Filipino worker's dilemma:

Uninjured, he is actually receiving "starvation wages";
injured, he receives a reduction, sometimes even an order of dis-
missal from his job. While it is true that some laborers may
exaggerate symptoms and prolong their illness, such cases can
only be rare, and to err on their side is much less of an injustice
to society than to err on the side of the employers who can easily
afford the pittance that these laborers receive.[8]

Unemployment

As might be expected of an agricultural country,
technological unemployment was still insignificant in the
Philippines. Among other types of unemployment, "residual unemployment" was by far the most common. With
complete lack of social insurance in general and unemployment compensation in particular, the unemployed were
a direct burden on the employed. In this respect the jobless
worker was worse off in the Philippines than in other countries where voluntary or compulsory schemes of unemployment compensation exist.

Unfortunately, available statistics on unemployment

[8] *Journal of the Philippine Medical Association*, August 1938.

are highly unsatisfactory. For example, according to official count, there were 1,184,080 unemployed persons throughout the country in 1935; four years later, the number of unemployed ten years of age or over had increased to 2,614,407. But we do not know how these figures were arrived at; and, considering the total number of employed persons in a normal year, it must be assumed that the Philippine official definition of "unemployment" is an unorthodox one. It certainly would seem improbable that in 1939 one out of every six persons in the total population was looking for wage employment and was unable to find it. And, faulty though they are, the figures for different years may be comparable. While in 1935 only 6,392 were registered as unemployed in the city of Manila, in 1939 the number had jumped to 154,135. But even such comparisons are unreliable unless we know that the methods used and the intensity of coverage were the same at different times. This does not seem to be the case, to judge from the rather astonishing result of a simple calculation: namely, that during four years of the Commonwealth regime the number of unemployed more than doubled for the country as a whole and increased nearly twenty-five times for the largest city in the country. It is, however, interesting to note that more than three-fifths of the unemployed listed agriculture as their usual field of employment; and the figures do reflect a tendency of the rural unemployed to migrate to Manila and other industrial and commercial centers in search of jobs.[9]

[9] According to the *Census of the Philippines*, 1939 (Vol. II, p. 821), 454,373 were classified as unable to work, and 664 failed to report whether they were able to work or not. Technically, therefore, the actual number of unemployed was less than 2,614,407. But this figure includes 1,761,214 persons between ten and nineteen years of age, many of whom were not looking for work at all. When 2,306,920 were reported as unemployed for more than 50 weeks, and 49,849 as unemployed for less than 10 weeks, we may conclude that large numbers of adults also are included who were not looking for employment. This conclusion is corroborated by the statement that 317,183 of the "unemployed" were 65 years of age and over and 535,463 were between 20 and 64. The working period of wage earners in the tropics does not extend

Sergio Bayan, an executive officer of the National Security Board, in 1939 summarized what seemed to him the major causes of unemployment in the Philippines as follows: (1) the presence of a great number of academically trained men and women looking for work in a field that is necessarily limited; (2) the disparity in the wages paid by the government and by private business; (3) the tendency of the people to flock to urban centers for better chances of employment, thus glutting the labor market in confined areas; and (4) the disruption of the national economy as a result of the world war and as a consequence of the economic provisions of the independence law.[10] Such generalizations as these are of little practical value, since each type of unemployment has its specific causes. In attacking the problem of unemployment in the Philippines, it is necessary to determine what types of unemployment exist and then to discover their causes.

Since there was no independent monetary system in the Philippines apart from that of the United States, the conventional methods of stabilization—changes in the discount rate, open market operations, etc.—could not be applied to the Philippines until the country acquired political independence and an independent monetary system with it.[11] However, it was within the power of the Common-

far beyond the thirties. Nevertheless, with appropriate social legislation, the residual supply of labor in the Philippines could be greatly reduced. If child labor were prohibited, more than a million potential wage earners would be taken out of the labor market. If there were a system of old-age security, the 317,183 jobless workers over 65 years of age would not be in the labor market, and the employment chances for those between 20 and 65 years of age would, at least in theory, be greatly increased.

[10] *Census of the Philippines*, 1939, Vol. II, p. 816.

[11] An economist familiar with Philippine finance takes issue with this statement. He does not believe that any direct connection can be established between unemployment and the monetary system of the Philippines. He writes: "The monetary system of the Philippines is independent, in spite of the fact that it is linked to the dollar and cannot be changed without the consent of the President of the United States. It is fully independent in that the circulation contracts and expands *pari passu* with changes in Philippine production, trade, and capital movement, and is not significantly

wealth Government to apply at least one of the corrective remedies for cyclical unemployment—a public-works program.[12] The limited extent of the practical relief which a public-works program gives was seen in the case of the province of Pangasinan, where while 900 laborers a day were employed by the local government 8,000 workers asked the Governor of the province for "immediate relief . . . . from hunger and starvation."[13]

Seasonal unemployment in the Philippines is primarily the result of the seasonal character of the country's major crops. Steady production and sales as methods of employment regularization were beyond the control of the Filipino producers, because they depended almost wholly upon the fluctuations of the American market which absorbed the bulk of Philippine export products. However, official encouragement was given the development of such "filler lines" as hat and basket weaving, textile weaving, fruit growing, poultry raising, and fishing, during the "off-season." Part-time work in these and other "filler lines" did help those who were subject to seasonal unemployment.

In 1938 the Department of Labor placed 1,632 applicants for employment, while six licensed private employment agencies placed 1,695 job seekers during the first half of that year. Some private agencies proved to be a "racket."[14] As a result, all the private agencies except the American Employment Agency were ordered closed.

---

influenced by corresponding movements in any other area. It may be assumed that the author has reference to the inability of the Philippines to adopt deficit financing to make work. If so, this inability would not arise from the monetary system but from the external and internal borrowing capacity of the Philippine government."

[12] An appropriation of ₱6,000,000 for public works projects was approved by the National Assembly in May 1938.

[13] *Manila Bulletin*, March 14, 1941.

[14] "Following numerous complaints filed with the Department of Labor charging private employment agencies with violation of . . . . the private Employment Agency Law, and the exposé made by metropolitan papers that girls recruited by these agencies ultimately land in houses of ill-repute,

Although, as we have seen, the available statistics seem greatly to exaggerate the extent of "residual unemployment," a better organization of the labor market would help to solve the unemployment problem of the extreme age groups in so far as it is real. If the size of the labor reserve is to be lessened, the majority of the unemployed workers under 20 and above 60 years of age must either be removed from the labor market or be given suitable jobs through a public-employment service.[15]

the Inspector-General of Labor . . . . conducted an investigation of four private employment agencies in the city of Manila" (*Labor Bulletin*, September 1939).

[15] The Unemployment Relief Unit of the Department of Labor functioned as a public employment service. The National Social Security Administration was created in August 1940 as the central public employment agency.

VI

THE LABOR MOVEMENT

History of Organization

The labor movement in the modern sense of the term is a relatively new development in the Philippines. When it did appear under the impetus of the factory system, it took a course somewhat different from that in other countries. Three hundred years of Spanish domination had made virtual slaves of the Filipino people. They were practically without political rights or civil liberties. It was this historical fact that shaped the Philippine labor movement in a way peculiar to a colony. The struggle against foreign domination and for political independence underlined even the most innocent demands of the Filipino workers and peasants. From the very outset the Philippine labor movement has thus been characterized by the political struggle for national liberation.

Under the Spanish regime peasant uprisings took place in 1622, 1629, 1660, 1744, 1823, 1844, and 1896. They were not, of course, inspired by organized labor movements. The 1896 uprising was led by the *Katipunan,* a secret revolutionary organization founded by the then police-hunted Andres Bonifacio, who later became a national hero. Although mainly political, the *Katipunan* had economic elements and is considered by some as a forerunner of the modern labor movement in the Philippines. In the last two decades of the nineteenth century there were frequent insurrections in the Philippines. It was against this revolutionary background that the *Katipunan* came into being.

Among more recent mass uprisings were the Tayug uprising of 1931, the Tangulan uprising of 1933, and the Sakdal uprising of 1935—all of them political, with only a background of agrarian unrest. These mass revolts were all poorly organized and did little more than indicate the existence of acute dissatisfaction in the country.

60

During the last half of the nineteenth century, two religious guilds and societies sprang up in the Philippines —the *Gremio de Obreros de Sampaloc* and the *Gremio de Escultores del Barrio de Santa Cruz*. These organizations were interested, not in social reform, but in the material and moral betterment of their members. The labor movement as we know it today started only at the turn of the century with the coming of American mercantilism into the Islands. The American occupation was a positive factor in the development of the factory system and hence of trade-unionism.

The first large trade-union to be organized under the American regime was the *Union Obrera Democrática Filipina*. Founded by Isabelo de los Reyes in Manila on February 2, 1902, it was composed of workers in lithographic and printing shops. It later grew into a federation called the *Union Democrática de las Filipinas*, including also workers of other trades. The union led an unsuccessful strike against the Manila Electric Railway and Light Company in 1903. The union president, Don Belong, was arrested and sentenced to serve four months in prison; the employers prevailed on the government to deport him later. A similar fate befell Dr. Dominador, the successor of Isabelo de los Reyes. The union subsequently collapsed.

However, the failure of the first labor union did not prevent the rise of others. In 1908 a cigar-workers' union called *Katubusan* was organized with the slogan, "The whole product of labor for the benefit of the workers." Another union at that time was the *Liga Obrera Filipina*, later known as the Federation of Labor of the Philippines. In 1913 the *Congreso Obrero de las Filipinas* was founded, and Hermando Cruz—later Secretary of Labor in the Commonwealth Government—became its first president. In the same year the Philippine Legislature declared May 1 a national holiday. It was on this occasion that the first labor congress was held in Manila. The congress passed resolutions demanding an eight-hour day, a labor law for the protection of children and women, an employers' liability law, and others.

The scope of the labor movement in the Philippines changed in response to changing economic conditions. During and after the first World War, Philippine industry developed rapidly, and with it also the labor movement. New avenues for employment were created by the new enterprises which sprang up to meet national and international requirements. A war boom was felt among sugar centrals, lumber mills, cement factories, coconut factories, oil mills, shoe factories, cigar and cigarette factories, breweries, distilleries, and land and water transportation companies. It was also a period of rising prices. However, labor unrest loomed large in the background of apparent material prosperity.

The *Federación del Trabajo de las Filipinas* was the first labor union to spring up in the midst of the war boom. It was organized on May 1, 1919. Almost simultaneously the *Pagkakaisa ng Magsasaka* (Union of Agricultural Tenants) was organized at Matungaw, Bulacan. The first congress of tenants and farm laborers was held in Manila in 1922. The upshot of the congress was the organization of the National Confederation of Farm Tenants and Laborers of the Philippines. The number of industrial disputes increased between the first World War and the world economic depression, as shown in Table IV listing disputes and workers involved in them between 1914 and 1929:

Organized labor swung into real action only after the Great Depression. When it started, a general feeling of insecurity had pacified the workers into relative inaction. But in 1933 the country began to feel the shock of the world-wide depression. Characteristically, business sought its way out through wage cuts. Labor could not long remain passive in the face of this widespread practice. As soon as market conditions began to improve, it agitated for the

maintenance of the existing wage scale and against further
wage cuts.

TABLE IV

NUMBER OF LABOR DISPUTES AND OF WORKERS INVOLVED, 1909–1938*

Year	Disputes	Workers Involved
1909	13	3,105
1910	5	222
1911	20	4,488
1912	11	2,880
1913	6	1,182
1914	10	1,017
1915	11	970
1916	17	4,485
1917	50	5,842
1918	84	16,289
1919	67	4,150
1920	68	11,139
1921	35	19,782
1922	24	14,956
1923	26	8,331
1924	20	6,784
1925	23	9,936
1926	27	7,279
1927	53	8,567
1928	38	4,729
1929	26	4,939
1930	36	6,096
1931	45	6,976
1932	31	4,396
1933	59	8,066
1934	63	17,662
1935	27	7,040
1936	51	5,649
1937	57	4,667
1938	125	20,426
1939†	222	28,104
1940†	158	18,728

* *Labor Bulletin*, September 1939.
† *Yearbook of Philippine Statistics, 1940*, Manila, 1941, p. 125.

From 1935 on, the labor movement experienced a
temporary setback, The unemployment situation had again
grown worse in the meantime, and this had the effect of

decreasing the labor turnover incident to strikes and lock-
outs. Thus, only 27 industrial disputes occurred in 1935,
the smallest number between 1930 and 1938. With the inauguration of the Commonwealth Government in 1935 and
with the subsequent adoption of a liberal labor policy, the
labor movement was given a fresh impetus. Business began to revive in 1936, and simultaneously the number of
strikes increased. As a result of improving employment
and other economic conditions more and more industrial
disputes arose in 1936 and thereafter.

The Philippine labor movement began to assume a more
militant and aggressive character with the introduction of
the Social Justice program by the government in 1937.
Organized labor lost no time in taking advantage of this
new deal for human rights as against property rights. Capital did not like this pro-labor trend of the government but
hoped it would lead to industrial peace. The government
expected to see the class struggle greatly tempered. But
organized labor was neither appeased nor pacified. On the
contrary, it turned more and more to the "left." Social
Justice now became the battle cry of the organized workers
and peasants in their struggle for economic security.

One of the progressive labor laws that was passed in the
spirit of the Social Justice program was Commonwealth Act
No. 183, commonly known as the Collective Bargaining
Law, the counterpart of the Wagner Law in the United
States. It gave labor an additional impetus to better its lot.
As Senator Wagner, author of the National Labor Relations
Act, correctly interpreted the apparent contradiction between increased labor unrest and the pro-labor policy of
the Roosevelt administration, Philippine labor became
bolder and more aggressive, "not in spite of but because
of"[1] the pro-labor policy of the Quezon administration.
And in 1939 industrial labor disputes reached the record-
breaking—but still not large—number of 222.

[1] *New York Times,* June 6, 1937.

Of 452 industrial disputes between 1935 and 1940, 153 unsettled cases were certified to the Court of Industrial Relations, and 344 disputes were sooner or later settled by the Department of Labor in favor of the workers.[2] Under the impact of the depression and under the resulting pro-labor policy of the government, the Philippine peasantry also was restless. In 1937 there were 633 tenant disputes. The number increased to 764 in 1938. Of this number, 592 were settled by the Department of Labor in favor of the tenants and 172 against them. Between 1937 and the middle of 1940, the Department of Labor settled 3,451 tenant disputes involving 9,840 tenant farmers, and of these cases, 2,671 were settled in favor of the tenant farmers.[3] Thus the number of tenant disputes invariably and greatly exceeds that of industrial disputes in the Philippines.[4]

Many of the disputes between landlords and tenants or between estate managements and wage laborers resulted in violent conflicts, and the latter in turn gave rise to armed intervention by the constabulary or the police. The display of force seemed to be a favorite pastime of some provincial governments. Under the guise of maintaining "law and order," the local police or the constabulary often broke up strikes or put down sabotage in the interest of the affected landlords or *hacenderos*. Such police partisanship only added fuel of class hatred and made for more violence.

Indicative of the progress of organized labor in the Philippines is the fact that the number of organized strikes in relation to that of spontaneous strikes increased from year to year.

The majority of labor disputes in the Philippines were caused by wage issues such as wage cuts, demands for wage increases, disputes over minimum wages, and wage rates,

[2] *Manila Bulletin*, March 25, 1941.

[3] *Ibid.*

[4] See also "Philippine Labor Policy in the Making," *Far Eastern Survey*, April 10, 1940, pp. 85–90.

and by demands for profit sharing or bonuses, old age pensions, vacations with pay, and salary standardization. Of the 487 industrial disputes between 1930 and 1938, 323 or 66.33 per cent concerned wages, while 164 or 33.67 per cent were on other issues. Where wages are legally set,

TABLE V

NUMBER OF ORGANIZED AND SPONTANEOUS STRIKES, 1930–1938*

Year	Organized Strikes	Spontaneous Strikes
1930	21	15
1931	29	16
1932	21	10
1933	38	21
1934	44	19
1935	25	2
1936	24	27
1937	23	27
1938	105	20

* *Manila Bulletin*, February 20, 1939.

disputes can of course be adjusted under the laws on which the rights are based. Those wage disputes which involve the violation of a labor contract are subject to arbitration, though the awards are not always enforceable. But if the wage system itself is at issue, disputes are subject to neither court decisions nor arbitration, since they involve the fundamental question of social relations in the capitalist system. Most wage disputes in the Philippines did not go as far as that, although the abolition of the wage system as such may sometimes be an implicit objective in other demands of radical organized labor.

The Department of Labor estimated that the eleven strikes from July 1 to December 31, 1940, cost the 2,721 workers involved a total loss of 10,233 working days and ₱12,592.50 in wages.[5] From the social point of view, strikes, whatever goals they may ultimately achieve, are a

[5] *Labor Bulletin*, January–February 1941.

source of industrial waste, involving, as they do, loss of labor time, loss of wages, loss of profits, sometimes loss of life, destruction of property, bitter antagonism, and inconvenience to the public. Nevertheless, strikes have been the weapon most readily available to Philippine labor in its struggle against capital. Sympathetic strikes were not uncommon. Even general strikes involving the industrial workers or agricultural laborers of several provinces occurred from time to time.

Many strikes failed to achieve the desired end, owing to lack of strike funds. Especially was this true in cases where the affected employer resorted to a retaliatory lockout. Labor unions preferred declaring a strike to submitting a labor dispute to mediation, for the latter takes too long for settlement. Furthermore, the result of government mediation, rendered through the Conciliation Service of the Department of Labor, may not always be satisfactory to labor.

As for the legality of the strike, the Court of Industrial Relations ruled that the "indiscriminate use of the strike as a weapon" by any labor union "cannot be countenanced."[6] The interpretation of the phrase "indiscriminate use" depends entirely on the social attitude of the judges of the Court of Industrial Relations. The implication seems to be that resort to mediation or arbitration rather than to a strike should be the rule.

Another important court decision bearing on the legality of strikes was handed down by the Philippine Supreme Court in the case of the *National Labor Union* vs. *The Philippine Match Company.* The Supreme Court declared that while the law recognizes "in a negative way" the workers' right to strike "it also creates all the means by which a resort thereto may be avoided," because "a strike is a remedy essentially coercive in character and

[6] *The Feltman Bros. Employees Association* vs. *The Feltman Bros. Import Co.,* August 22, 1939.

general in its disturbing effects upon the social order and the public interests." It ruled further that "a resort thereto by laborers shall be deemed a choice of a remedy peculiarly their own, and outside of the statute, and as such, they must accept all the risks attendant upon their choice," and that "if they succeed and the employer succumbs, the law will not stand in their way in the enjoyment of the lawful fruits of their victory." But the Court warned that "if they fail, they cannot thereafter invoke the protection of the law from the consequences of their conduct, unless the right they wished vindicated is one which the law will, by all means, protect and enforce."[7]

On the other hand, the unionist attitude toward the strike is well characterized by the following statement of Socialist leader Pedro Abad Santos:

Strike is the most effective, if not the only, weapon of struggle of the working class for its emancipation. The workers can never rely on what the government intends to do for them, for no capitalist government can give the workers their own. They have to struggle and fight, and the strike is their best weapon. In his last message to the National Assembly, President Quezon, while blaming capital for not fully realizing its obligation to labor and society, asserts that strikes are unnecessary in the Philippines, where the government, he says, is earnestly endeavoring to help labor in its just claims. I wish that may be true, but it is the experience of labor anywhere that a government is but the executive committee of the ruling class and that labor must fight and struggle to get concessions even from the most benevolent government of a capitalist state . . . . But President Quezon's attitude toward strike is not to be wondered at. While it is true that the President has in several instances shown himself a friend of labor, yet the inescapable fact is that he, as head of the government, is the representative of the ruling capitalist class that fears strikes—for a strike is a small revolution.[8]

In the Philippines the legality of picketing, boycott, and sabotage was interpreted *pari passu* with that of the

---

[7] *The National Labor Union* vs. *The Philippine Match Company.* See *Manila Bulletin*, June 28, 1940.

[8] Convocation address, University of the Philippines, February 1, 1940.

strike. Since the right of collective bargaining was no longer in question in the Philippines, the discriminate use of the strike and any other means that tends to strengthen industrial democracy should be protected as legitimate rights.

Labor Organization

Trade-unionism had not yet reached the broad masses in the Philippines in 1941. The great majority of unorganized workers and peasants, according to Francisco Varona, late technical assistant to the Philippine Resident Commissioner in the United States, were between the devil of illiteracy and the deep sea of apathy. This is not surprising in view of the fact that more than half the population of the Philippines is illiterate.[9] While in more advanced countries labor was fighting for its rights, in the Philippines the majority of workers were utterly ignorant of their rights. They felt that they were exploited but were helpless in the face of powerful employers. In desperation they rebelled against whatever and whomever they believed to be the cause of their suffering, but not in an organized manner. Only slowly did the laboring masses learn from their bitter experience the value of organization, and still more slowly the methods to effect it.

The status of organized labor in the Philippines may be seen from Table VI (p. 70) of registered labor unions.[10] On December 31, 1939, there was a total of 351 recognized labor unions (169 independent, 182 chapters) with a total membership of 84,013 workers.[11] At the end of 1940, there were 391 registered labor organizations with a total

[9] *Census of the Philippines*, 1939.

[10] Section I of Commonwealth Act No. 213 defines a legitimate labor union as "an organization, association, or union of laborers duly registered and permitted to operate by the Department of Labor and governed by a constitution and by-laws not repugnant to or inconsistent with the laws of the Philippines."

[11] *Labor Bulletin*, May–June, 1904, p. 211.

membership of 96,877.[12] In the same year, the number of
organized workers, industrial and agricultural, in *unregis-
tered* labor unions was estimated at 190,000. In other
words, some 286,877 out of 5,319,173 gainfully employed
workers, or roughly 5 per cent, were organized; but only
1.8 per cent of the labor population was *legitimately*
organized.

TABLE VI

GROWTH OF LABOR ORGANIZATION, 1918–1934*

Year	Unions	Membership
1918	143	147,331
1919	31	42,006
1920	87	63,652
1921	99	61,935
1922	97	68,976
1923	118	70,548
1924	145	89,826
1925	122	83,544
1926	119	62,858
1927	103	63,716
1928	110	68,828
1929	114	62,366
1930	122	78,781
1931	110	96,041
1932	116	?
1933	135	13,109
1934	122	72,613

* Department of Labor figures, cited by B. Abellera in *History of Organized Labor in the Philippines*, University of the
Philippines, Manila, 1938.

The latest available analysis of trade-unions by industries (end of 1940) showed the following distribution of
the total number of 391 registered labor organizations:
sugar centrals and refineries headed the list of industries
with 42 trade-unions, involving 21,616 workers; land
transportation accounted for 47 unions with a total membership of 8,897; in mining there were 25 unions with
15,106 members; in stevedoring, there were 34 unions,
with 8,341 members; in coconut- and vegetable-oil indus-

[12] *Yearbook of Philippine Statistics, 1940*, p. 129.

Photo by Fenno Jacobs, from Three Lions

Shelling coconuts at the Furukawa Plantation. This is a desiccated
coconut plant near Davao.

tries, 11 unions with 3,021 members; in cigar and cigarette factories, 10 unions with 2,702 members; also farmers had 19 unions, with a membership of 3,887.[13]

"Most industrial and commercial firms in the Philippines practiced "open-shop" policies. Some even imposed the "yellow-dog" contract on the employees. It is significant that organized labor had penetrated such key industries as foodstuffs, transportation and communications, and public utilities, so that in case of a general strike organized labor was in a position to paralyze, at least temporarily, the whole industrial system.

Among the registered organizations, the largest was the National Labor Union, with a total membership of 8,490. It had 44 branches in and around Manila, involving workers in numerous trades, occupations, and industries. Antonio D. Paguia, the "strike king," headed this organization and was also a member of the presidium of the Collective Labor Movement, a radical federation of labor unions. The second largest was the Philippine Labor Union, with a total membership of 8,257. Esteban I. Vasquez was its president and was also a leader of the National Federation of Labor, a conservative federation of labor unions.[14] The third largest labor organization was the *Federación Obrera de las Filipinas*, with a total membership of 5,626. It concentrated its activity in the southern provinces, José M. Nava, its president, was at the same time chairman of the presidium of the Collective Labor Movement. The next in the list was the *Federación Obrera de la Industria Tabaquera de las Filipinas*, with a total membership of 2,405. Isabelo Tejada headed it and was also a leader of the Collective Labor Movement.

[13] *Ibid.*, p. 130.

[14] Lest it be thought that the labor and independence movements are identical, it may be observed in passing that Mr. Vasquez and the National Federation of Labor were opposed to independence in 1946 and supported the movement for indefinite continuation of the Commonwealth form of government.

Besides recognized labor organizations, there were a number of large and small associations of workers and farm tenants which were either unrecognized officially or were indifferent to registration. Outstanding among them were: the General Workers Union, under Socialist leadership, with a membership of about 50,000; the Philippine Confederation of Peasants, under Communist leadership, with some 60,000 members; and the *Kapisapan Ng Anak Pawis* (Sons of Sweat), under Communist leadership, with about 80,000 members. These and other radical labor unions were often more powerful in influence and larger in number than registered unions. Of the radical unions under Communist influence the late Francisco Varona is reported to have said: "The Communists are the best organizers in point of efficiency, organization, discipline and sincerity."[15] The Communist-Socialist influence was strong in the provinces of Pampanga, Nueva Ecija, and Bulacan, while the Sakdal wielded great influence in Laguna.

There were also a few company unions organized by employers on the basis of "welfare capitalism." However, company unions were unpopular among the workers and often got into jurisdictional disputes with outside labor unions. For example, 39 workers of the Central Luzon Milling Company at Bamban, Tarlac, were dismissed for their refusal to affiliate with the Central Luzon Union, a company union headed by the Central manager, Modesto Cortabitarte. "Only the timely intervention of Mayor Marcelo Sibal of Bamban prevented an armed clash" between the management and the dismissed workers, who were determined to fight for reinstatement.[16]

"Horizontal" unions prevailed among drivers, chauffeurs, hotel workers, printers, shoe and slipper makers, carpenters, mechanics, clerks, and salesmen. In the industrial centers, "vertical" unions were gaining ground,

[15] *Kalayan*, Manila, December 12, 1938.
[16] *Manila Bulletin*, November 15, 1938.

involving all the workers of a given industry regardless of trade or craft. The workers of tobacco, mining, lumber and timber, transportation and communications, public utilities, manufacturing industries, and sugar centrals were vertically organized. Lack of large-scale enterprises and absence of vertical monopolies accounted for the prevalence of horizontal trade-unionism.

Unionization will doubtless develop *pari passu* with industrialization. However, Japan, with its notorious anti-labor policy, dominated the Philippines for three years. During the Japanese occupation there was little hope for labor organization. Any union activities, open or underground, were obliged to remain under a ban. The Japanese would probably have made a cat's-paw of a pro-Japanese section of the working class, the Ganap party (formerly known as the Sakdal party), in an attempt to pacify the restive Filipino masses. At this writing it is not known what concessions the Japanese felt themselves obliged to give to the Filipino working class for political expediency. The chances are that the political character of the Philippine labor movement will be strengthened by the Japanese suppression of conventional trade-union actions. We may assume that Philippine labor will once again engage in a struggle for national freedom in the postwar reconstruction of economic life.

Philippine organized labor has much to hope for in the postwar era. The democratic tradition which America has implanted in the Philippines is conducive to the healthy growth of the labor movement. The assured right of collective bargaining is a sound step in the direction of industrial democracy. Unlike its tendency in some other countries, capital in the Philippines has not become vicious and repressive in any organized way toward labor. Labor spying, union busting, and other anti-labor practices have not gained ground in the country. Another favorable factor is the liberal labor policy of the government. As long as the government sticks to its Social Justice program, organized labor can hope to make headway.

The potentially most important factor is the long-range program of industrialization. Industrial unionism presupposes the development of industry. More than anything else, industrialization will prepare the ground for the rapid growth of industrial unionism in the Philippines; for, as experience shows, industrial unionism alone can reach the broad mass of unorganized workers. Indeed, labor organization is destined to be "the vehicle for the transplanting of the democratic doctrine into industry, and collective bargaining the machinery for its operation."[17]

Labor Partisanship

At the 1929 convention of the Philippine Labor Congress the labor movement was definitely split into right- and left-wing camps as the labor leaders took sides either with Crisanto Evangelista, the Communist leader, or with Ruperto S. Cristobal, a conservative laborite. Ever since then the labor front in the Philippines has been characterized by factionalism and partisanship. There is not yet any basic unity on the labor front, although a measure of superficial compromise between the conservative and the radical sides is observable.

There were three national federations of labor in the Philippines, controlling or influencing the policies of nearly three hundred labor unions. One was the National Federation of Labor, organized in 1935 by Cristobal, then private secretary to the Secretary of Labor. Some sixty-five conservative unions were affiliated with the N.F. of L. Another federation of the conservative type was the Confederated Workers' Alliance, the C.W.A. Together with the N.F. of L., it led the right wing of organized labor. The last and newest federation was the Collective Labor Movement, commonly known as C.L.M., with which some

[17] J. Rosenfarb, *The National Labor Policy*, New York, 1934.

seventy-six radical and liberal unions were affiliated. The C.L.M., by far the largest national federation in the country, led the left camp of the labor front.

Under the stimulus of the C.I.O. movement in America and under the inspiration of the Social Justice program of the government at home, the radical Filipino labor leaders made concerted efforts to popularize the ideal of labor unity; but they failed to bring the conservative labor leaders to a united front. One attempt after another failed and only widened the gap between the right and the left labor camps. Early in 1938 President Quezon suggested labor unity in his conference with labor leaders at Malacañan Palace. Nothing of importance came of the conference. In February of the same year the Secretary of Labor delegated Assemblymen Felipe José and Enrique Magalona to discuss the possibilities of labor unity with some Manila labor leaders. On March 2, 1938, nine presidents and authorized representatives of important labor unions met in Manila and approved a resolution endorsing the plan of Assemblyman Magalona for the organization of a Committee on Labor Organization. The plan was given much publicity, but it failed to accomplish its purpose. Thus the first attempt to achieve labor unity from above failed.

Shortly after a successful May Day parade and demonstration in 1938, about twenty-five labor leaders met in Manila and succeeded in forming the framework of a Collective Labor Movement. This caused an exchange of accusations and counter-accusations between conservative and radical labor leaders, and aggravated the situation so much that the new attempt at labor unity appeared to the public to have collapsed. The upshot of the stormy feud was described in a Manila paper as follows:

On the labor front these days, one hears mostly nothing but mutual accusations of "racketeering," charges and counter-charges that this or that labor leader is "the worst enemy of labor" because he "sells out to the capitalists" after having lived handsomely on the dues paid by the rank and file of his union.

The quarrel became so bitter the other day that union leaders, holding a conference under the auspices of the CLM, split into left and right wings after a rather acrimonious exchange of compliments. Among the epithets bandied about during the brief congress were "traitor," "betrayer of the working class," "racketeer," and so forth.

The majority of the unions having decided to stick to the CLM, the right-wing groups promptly announced a "counter-convention" wherein, it was darkly hinted, the leftist leaders will not only be challenged to prove their accusations but will also be accused of more heinous offenses. And in the manner of all reactionary groups everywhere, an unusually futile right-wing union issued a statement to the press saying that "the CLM is merely the camouflage to a campaign to spread Communism in the Philippines."[18]

At a labor congress held in Manila on June 26, 1938, over 3,000 workers from radical and liberal unions formally established the Collective Labor Movement, affecting 1,800,000 persons throughout the country, or over a third of the total labor population. The congress "declared war" on the conservative labor unions, passed a resolution withdrawing confidence in the Department of Labor for "unjust treatment of labor," endorsed President Quezon's Social Justice program, and signed a labor pact. This pact included: (1) recognition of the autonomy of labor organization; (2) intensification of the campaign for higher wages, shorter working weeks, and better working conditions; (3) expurgation of "scabism" in all its forms; (4) co-operation with the government in the settlement of strikes and labor disputes; and (5) agitation for the liberalization of government policy regarding permits for peaceful assembly. Most of the key positions in the presidium of the C.L.M. were held by Communist and Socialist leaders.

Thus unity within the ranks of radical and liberal unionists became a reality through the formation of the Collective Labor Movement. However, this unity was not

18 *Herald Mid-Week Magazine,* June 6, 1938.

inclusive, for the conservative elements were still left out. At least it may serve as the starting point for complete labor unity in the Philippines.

On August 28 and 29, 1938, an "anti-Communist" labor convention was held in Manila under the auspices of the National Federation of Labor. As compared with the 3,000 delegates to the convention of the C.L.M. held two months before, only 983 delegates were present at this "anti-Communist" rally. However, this "rightist" convention had the official support of President Quezon, former Secretary of Labor Torres, and the former Mayor of Manila, Posadas. Its real motive seems to have been to discredit the radical leadership of the C.L.M. The resolution passed at this convention reveals the nature and meaning of reactionary labor organization. It reads in part:

> Whereas, communism is vitally undermining the real foundation of an intelligent, responsible, and honest labor movement in the Philippines by organizing units designed to defeat nationalism and Filipinism among the Filipino laborers, by implanting the seeds of class hatred and struggle, by adopting new tactics of boring from within, through known communistic leaders who joined and adhered to labor unions and organizations only with the view of introducing the same communistic ideas and principles inconsistent with those of democratic and republican forms of government;
>
> Whereas, we sincerely believe that communism as a movement is unpatriotic and anti-Filipino because it is against the ideas and ideals of Filipino heroes who have sacrificed their lives in order to set their mother country free from internal strife and political bondage, and because it does not recognize the Filipino flag as the symbol of Filipino idealism, the only flag respected and recognized by them being that of communism and Soviet Russia which symbolizes revolution and class struggle;
>
> Therefore, be it resolved as it is hereby resolved, that communism in all its aspects, as a political, economic, and sociological experiment, be condemned, it being a source of danger to a responsible, intelligent and honest labor movement in the Philippines; and an unremitting and an uncompromising vigilance be

hereby declared against any encroachment by persons imbued with communistic tenets and ideals.[19]

In the meantime, radical unionists went ahead to consolidate their position, avoiding open conflict with the conservative unionists. Almost as a prelude to the compromise between the right- and left-wing labor groups that was to come a few months later, the Communist and Socialist parties held a three-day joint convention in Manila in November 1938 and declared their formal merger. Pertinent among numerous demands made in the resolution passed at this convention are the following:

1. Recognition of all trade unions and the rights of collective bargaining; non-recognition of company unions by the government

2. A floor for wages and a ceiling for hours—a decent minimum wage and the maximum 8-hour day and 44-hour week in industry and commerce, including farms and plantations employing more than 10 farm laborers

3. Full enforcement of the existing compensation and industrial safety and sanitation laws

4. Large-scale public works program to give work to unemployed unproductive peasants, city poor, school graduates, and professionals

. . . .

6. Establishment of a system of adequate old-age pensions, disability, and sickness benefits for all employees of the government and its institutions

7. Strict enforcement of the rice tenancy law and the anti-usury law through co-operation of the government agencies with the peasant organizations

8. Prevention of land grabbing and arbitrary evictions of tenants and small landowners for debts, failure to pay taxes, activities in the tenant societies

9. Establishment of a system of government credit for small production loans to tenants and small landowners to take the place of usurious loans advanced by landowners and merchants

[19] *Labor Bulletin*, August 1938.

10. Establishment of government-controlled, co-operative marketing associations for small producers

. . . .

15. Fullest guarantee of the right of free speech, assembly, and
the press, for all citizens

. . . .

18. Restrictions upon and outlawing of any party, group, or
clique, or any conspiracy under the direction of a foreign
power, which aims to undermine, weaken, or destroy civil
rights and the institutions of democracy

. . . .

20. Extension of the government housing program to all slum
areas

. . . .

22. Reduction of taxes on small properties, of license fees of
those newly engaged in professions and business; increase
of taxes, on a graduated scale, on corporations, inherit-
ances and the higher incomes; and approval of luxury
taxes

. . . .

24. Immediate utilization of government surpluses and unex-
pended appropriations for purposes of relief, public works,
and social welfare measures

25. Government ownership of all public utilities, such as power,
water supply, transportation, and radio.[20]

These demands stand in sharp relief against the accusations of the conservative unionists embodied in their
resolution passed at the "anti-Communist" convention.

The war between the right and left wings of the Philippine labor movement was described in a popular magazine
as follows:

At no other time did labor leaders for various groups work
off more bile than in 1938. The right-wing groups hurled sly
charges of communism at the radical, newly organized Collective
Labor Movement. Right-wing meetings, always well attended
both by laborers and ranking government officials, had over half
of their time devoted to the exclusive pastime of denouncing the
aggressive Left, and expressing their horror over the possible

[20] *Manila Bulletin*, November 1, 1938.

consequences lending undue impetus to insidious pink propaganda. The charges of the right-wing labor leaders were no less vehement than those of ranking government officials who were invited to confirm their beliefs.

The mortality rate among right-wing labor leaders, however, was appallingly high. If they could not exert enough effort to grab the fleshpots of labor leadership, they yoked themselves into government service and there insisted on their status as labor leaders of an even more respectable character.

The left wing had very few wounds to lick. They hurled investives at the right-wing groups with as much gusto, called them mercenaries, reactionaries, tools of capitalists, and racketeers. A lot of time was used in such dissipating pastimes.[21]

Perspective

A bitter struggle for supremacy went on between the conservative N.F. of L. and C.W.A. on the one hand and the radical C.L.M. on the other until about the middle of 1939. It looked for a while as if labor unity were hopeless. Then on June 5, 1939, nearly a year after the establishment of the Collective Labor Movement, some 200,000 workers participated in "one of the biggest labor demonstrations ever seen in the city of Manila," to celebrate formal labor unity. President Quezon participated in the labor jubilee by making a speech before the workers. He reiterated his Social Justice program and voiced the sentiments already cited:

> Labor is more important than capital. Labor is the original producer of wealth, whether individual or national. Without labor, wealth cannot be produced and the already accumulated wealth will be consumed and disappear. Without capital, labor can't produce wealth and in time accumulate it . . . The rights of labor are more important than the rights of capital because the rights of labor are human rights, whereas the rights of capital are property rights.

On May 22, 1939, a National Commission of Labor was created under the sponsorship of the Secretary of

[21] *Graphic*, Manila, May 25, 1939.

Labor, and the three rival federations of labor were temporarily united in it. A "Labor Pact" was signed by the delegates of these federations of labor composing the Commission. The text of the Pact throws light on the nature of the united labor front. It reads:

The labor organizations in the Philippines duly represented in a meeting held this 22nd of May, 1939, have agreed to create a supreme body to be known as the National Commission of Labor, which henceforth shall constitute an organization symbolizing labor unity in the Philippines.

This National Commission of Labor shall be composed of thirty members, which shall be equally apportioned to the following three major labor groups: the Collective Labor Movement, the Federacion Nacional del Trabajo, and the Confederated Workers' Alliance. This Commission shall be temporarily presided over by the Secretary of Labor as the supreme head thereof.

The National Commission of Labor shall strive to carry out the following:

(1) Strict maintenance of unity among all labor organizations in the Philippines;

(2) Intervention in matters regarding the conflicts arising between laborers and labor organizations and between organizations and employers; and

(3) Adoption of all such rules, regulations, and principles to govern the activities of the National Commission of Labor, which shall be binding upon all labor organizations constituting the National Commission of Labor.[22]

On May 29, 1939, in the office of the Secretary of Labor, the charter governing the activities of the National Commission of Labor and the relations among its members was approved and signed by the delegates of the composite labor groups. The principal objective of the Commission, as defined by the charter, was to "promote harmony and foster mutual assistance and co-operation among labor organizations in the Philippines, and to co-ordinate their movements relating to the economic, social, cultural and moral improvement of the working people."[23]

[22] *Labor Bulletin*, May 1939.   [23] *Ibid.*

Thus the radical and conservative labor organizations were brought together in a united front for the first time in the history of the Philippine labor movement. Although formal in nature, this unity was the first concrete step toward trade-union unity in the Islands.

Under the impetus of the formation of the National Commission of Labor a National Commission of Peasants was created, also with the Secretary of Labor as temporary chairman. According to the constitution adopted, the basic objectives of the Commission of Peasants were "to maintain peasant unity in the Philippines, to uphold and defend the rights and interests of tenants, farm hands, and small landowners, within the pale of law and order, and to promote and co-ordinate all such activities as will redound to the social, economic, cultural and moral improvement of the peasant citizenry and the rural communities in the Philippines." The inclusion of the phrase "within the pale of law and order" in the constitution of the National Commission of Peasants is as significant as is its absence in the charter of the National Commission of Labor. On July 16, 1939, a huge crowd of rural workers turned out to participate in the unity celebration of the National Commission of Peasants at Cabanatuan, Nueva Ecija. President Quezon was present at this celebration also and delivered a congratulatory speech. But a well-known Communist leader, Juan Feleo, was unanimously chosen as executive secretary of the Commission.[24]

Internal dissension loomed large within the National Commission of Labor, while unity within the National Commission of Peasants remained intact. This was probably because the former represented a loose unity of ideologically and politically conflicting labor groups. A metropolitan paper had this observation to make:

When Labor in the Philippines celebrates Labor Day today, it will be its first celebration as one homogeneous unit under a

[24] *Manila Bulletin*, July 17, 1939.

single standard—and probably its last. For today marks the
rekindling of old rivalries and petty jealousies among labor
leaders who were united by Secretary of Labor José Avelino
under the National Commission of Labor only 348 days ago
. . . . Secretary Avelino said his resignation (as chairman of
the Commission) is due to the fact that he believes the Commissions are now able to take care of themselves. But hardly
had he uttered the sentence when labor leaders started jockeying
for the position to control the organizations. Significantly, Communists and radicals seem to have the upper hand.[25]

Unlike that in highly industrialized countries, the labor
movement in the Philippines was not strictly a movement
of industrial workers. Rather it was composed of a mixture
of industrial workers and peasants. In the background of
day-to-day economic struggles, the general struggle against
precapitalistic remnants of labor relations and for a fair
system of industrialism loomed large. The political level
of the Philippine labor movement rose, for organized labor
was not only demanding higher wages and other concessions but was beginning to challenge the whole system of
landlordism and free enterprise.

Frederico Mangahas, popular Manila columnist, made
a rather penetrating analysis of the labor outlook in the
Philippines, as follows:

While workers elsewhere unite and organize and drive toward a determined and definite goal, dying a thousand heroic
deaths for economic opportunity and freedom, Philippine labor
all along has been content to meet and banquet annually, listen
to a solemn speech of the Secretary of Capital, and wrangle on
the next batch of officers to collect fees and graduate ultimately
into a government job. Thus instead of making politics serve
labor, labor wittingly or unwittingly lends itself to be an un-
mitigated slave of politics. Instead of developing a technique
for effective organization as observed in the theory and practice
of successful labor movements elsewhere, Philippine labor nour-
ishes a parasitic heterogeneous leadership that buoys itself up on
ancient and outmoded abstractions of social justice, willing to
trade or connive with the first to come with a proposal . . . .

[25] *Manila Bulletin*, May 1, 1940.

Philippine labor need not grope any more for inspiration. The world is one battleground today in which its cause is being fought, and it is not lacking for champions; for dignity, heroism and power are now household words.[26]

Sarcastic as it is, Mangahas' criticism is valid, on the whole. Sincere labor leaders would undoubtedly welcome such biting yet really sympathetic criticism for the advancement of their cause. Labor leaders will come and go, but those labor organizations which have a record of advancing the cause of labor, regardless of political partisanship, will probably remain and become more successful.

It was, of course, impossible to maintain labor gains during the Japanese occupation of the Islands, for labor as well as capital was regimented to suit the occupying power. However, the Japanese occupation may well have had the effect of strengthening labor unity, not on economic but on political grounds. At any rate, the Japanese were not able to destroy the democratic tradition that has become an integral part of the Philippine labor movement. If the economic dislocations which the war has occasioned should coincide with the disappearance of a favorable American market for Philippine products, the condition of the masses may become considerably worse and social unrest may become even more intense. Under such circumstances it is conceivable that the government and business may wage a united war against labor, as has happened in the Fascist countries. But as long as it can do so Philippine labor will minimize the danger of regimentation and oppression by compelling both government and business to make further commitments along the lines of political and industrial democracy. If the various labor groups sink their ideological and political differences while facing the urgent task of defending their common interests and rights, there is no reason why Philippine labor should not face the future with confidence.

[26] *Tribune*, Manila, January 16, 1938.

VII

CONCLUSION

Before Pearl Harbor the solution of the so-called "agrarian problem" constituted the major concern of the Philippine government and the Filipino people. There were before them various and conflicting proposals and measures for the solution of this paramount question, ranging from mild reforms to the outright nationalization of the land.

All the agrarian reforms of the government were correlated directly with the Social Justice program. For instance, in 1938, the government leased the huge Buenavista estate in the province of Bulacan and converted it into a national laboratory for co-operative experiments. The management was in the hands of the government, which furnished worthy tenant farmers with cheap credit and seeds and tools at cost. The management taught them scientific farming, hygiene, and proper recreation. Up to the outbreak of the war, according to reports, the experiment had been favorably received by the tenant farmers. The notable feature of the experiment was the fact that the tenant farmers were freed from the hardships of high land rent, usurious interest, and personal abuses to which they had been subjected before.

Another interesting agrarian measure was the establishment in 1939 of the National Land Resettlement Administration for the purpose of promoting land ownership and agricultural development. The plan was to accommodate at least half a million people in Mindanao in ten years.[1]

Settlements were to be organized on a "producer-consumer basis." This was a concrete step toward the utilization of the public domain for agricultural progress as well

---

[1] For a detailed account of this land settlement program and its initial results, see Karl J. Pelzer, *Pioneer Settlement in the Asiatic Tropics* (Institute of Pacific Relations, New York, 1945).

as for the partial solution of the agrarian problem. But the Japanese occupation put an end to all that, and that movement cannot at once resume large proportions.

In addition to these public agrarian reforms, the Socialist experiment on collective farming in Pampanga deserves mention. The General Workers' Union, under Socialist leadership, leased a large tract of privately owned land for sugar-cane cultivation on a collective basis. Reports from various sources indicate that the Socialist plan adopted in this particular instance was highly successful. It was hoped that the success of this collective farm might stimulate similar ventures in other provinces. It differed from the Buenavista plan of the government in that, while the tenancy system was preserved in the latter case, the Pampanga tenant farmers, through their union, were placed in direct control of the land and of the disposal of the produce.

The government also launched a campaign for the organization and promotion of consumers' co-operatives with a view to increasing the native share in Philippine retail trade. In October 1938 the Consumers' Co-operative League was founded, and Saturnino R. Mendinueto, chief of the Trade Promotion Division of the Bureau of Commerce, was elected its president. In June 1939 there were thirty-four consumers' co-operatives with a total membership of 5,000. Together with credit, marketing, and producers' co-operatives, the newly organized consumers' co-operatives were expected to promote what Secretary of Finance Roxas has called a "producer-consumer" economy preparatory for political independence. Like similar movements elsewhere, the co-operative movement in the Philippines has contributed little toward the solution of labor problems, for in its present state of development it is neither a substitute for a profit economy nor an alternative to a planned collective economy.

One of the greatest achievements of the Social Justice program, as far as the peasantry is concerned, was its

Crushing the sugar cane to extract the juice

American machinery makes sugar, the most important export
commodity of the Philippine Commonwealth

stimulation of peasant unity. There are diverse opinions concerning the motives that prompted the establishment of the National Commission of Peasants. Some say that it was organized to offset the genuine agrarian movement in Pampanga and to support the re-election of a conservative provincial governor. Whatever the intention, the effect was a public recognition on the part of the government that the organization of agricultural workers is in the interest of the state and that through organization they are better able than the government to solve some of their pressing problems. Naturally the government, through its Social Justice program, tried not only to conquer reaction but also to encourage the more constructive rather than the most radical elements among the organized workers. Sometimes this gave the program a semblance of compromise and even of substitution of exceedingly moderate for more fundamental demands. Nevertheless, to make any kind of peasant organization respectable is a step in advance. Its encouragement will have a more far-reaching effect upon the condition of the rural masses than the establishment of an Agricultural and Industrial Bank, co-operatives, land settlements, or other public measures.

Likewise, official encouragement and promotion of labor organization in industry must be esteemed a creditable partial embodiment of the Social Justice program. The creation of the Court of Industrial Relations, the enactment of the Collective Bargaining Law and of the new Eight-Hour Labor Law, the establishment of the National Social Security Administration, and other measures were all to the advantage of labor. An interesting sidelight on the labor policy of the Commonwealth Government and of the Quezon administration was the granting of pardons to leaders of the Tangulan and Sakdal uprisings, and similar evidences of liberalism. These gestures were accepted by the workers as genuine installments of pro-labor policy, even though in other matters the government showed its

willingness to use repressive measures in situations where
the maintenance of law and order was at stake.

It is difficult to put one's finger on any one thing as the
"realization" of the Social Justice program. The fact of
the matter is that many different things were done in the
name of that principle. Yet the consequences were often
at variance with the motive. One of the obvious difficulties
was that the whole program of Social Justice was centered
around the personality of President Quezon. There is no
assurance that the program will be carried on by his suc-
cessors. Another difficulty was the fact that inside as well
as outside the government there were too many who inten-
tionally or unintentionally sabotaged the program.

The Social Justice program, in fact, faces a dilemma.
On the one hand, it inspires labor to assert its rights; on
the other, it tries to preserve "the integrity of private
property." It may reach a point where it can no longer
reconcile the conflicting interests of capital and labor.
Then the Social Justice administration may have to seek
a way out of the impasse in one form of collectivism or
another—the corporate national economy of Fascism or
the collective economy of Socialism. The course of events
may yet force the Philippines from its successful start of
gradual evolution into a more painful and disturbing social
revolution.

Industrialization for home consumption was initiated
as a national program with a view to preparing the country
for political independence. Much depends on whether or
not preferential trade relations with the United States will
be prolonged. If they are terminated, as provided by the
Independence Act, then industrialization on a "producer-
consumer" basis should by all means be encouraged. However, industrialization along the line of autarchy or self-
sufficiency—in the writer's opinion, not shared by every
student of the matter—is as unsound economically as it
is dangerous politically. In a peaceful and free world, no

country would have to hide behind a wall of self-sufficiency; for the world's resources would be exchanged according to needs and ability to buy. In any case, the Philippine program of industrialization will have to be adjusted to postwar world economic conditions. However, the basic purpose of "raising the standard of living of the whole people" should ever be the guiding principle of Philippine industrialization. The postwar economic reconstruction of the country will, in all likelihood, require economic planning more deliberate in purpose, more central in control, and more comprehensive in scope than such planning has been thus far. No rules can be set down regarding the re-allocation of the country's resources for postwar production and consumption. Suffice it to say that Philippine industrialization will have to follow the dictates of social economy rather than those of political expediency.

As far as agrarian reforms are concerned, most of the prewar measures should be continued, particularly the better utilization of the public domain, the encouragement of scientific farming, co-operative experiments, and the organization (unionization) and education of the rural masses. Other methods should be added as demanded by the postwar requirements of the country and in response to the world's changing economic conditions. Here again the basic aim should be the strengthening of the people's security and the raising of the plane of living.

It would be to the advantage of the whole nation as well as to that of the agricultural population to increase the productivity of agricultural labor. Agricultural development along the line of "subsistence farming," combined with the raising of profitable money crops—as envisioned by the National Land Resettlement Administration—should help the rural masses in the long run. As the home market develops and mass purchasing power increases with it, the production of money crops, apart from its effect upon the welfare of their producers, will become a matter of practical business and national revenue. "Subsistence farming" as such in the Philippine setting is no more progressive than the "back-to-the-farm" movement was in America, for it looks back to those "good old days" when every peasant was more or less self-sufficient and, in theory, enjoyed a measure of economic security. The general aims of agricultural reforms in the Philippines should be directed toward eliminating the existing relics of pre-capitalistic exploitation—the traditional forms of landlordism, insecure tenure, usury—and at such positive measures as greater equality in land ownership, greater productive efficiency, and higher levels of living for the rural masses. Furthermore, rural reconstruction should be co-ordinated with industrialization in a general economic plan.

Postwar industrial expansion in the Philippines, as elsewhere, largely because of capital replacements and technological innovations, will have a favorable effect upon investment, output, and employment. As world trade returns to normalcy, the Philippine economy should be able to raise its standard of consumption considerably, even in the absence of a protected American market. But regardless of future economic relations with other countries, the material welfare of Philippine labor depends largely upon internal changes, particularly as to production and distribution. If national output is increased through improved methods and means of production, and if distribution of wealth and income becomes more equal through such measures as a progressive income tax, increased public spending for social security, and minimum wage laws, there is no reason why the Filipino people should not enjoy an increasingly higher scale of living.

The Social Justice program, when it can be resumed, will doubtless continue to be promoted through planning for the general welfare and for the economic welfare of the laboring masses in particular. The democratic tradition which the American regime has instituted in the Philippines is conducive to a satisfactory solution of labor problems. Given political democracy in the form of representative government, common suffrage, and civil liberties, as the Philippines enjoyed these before the war, organized labor will be instrumental in realizing its economic counterpart, viz., economic democracy, in the sense of equal access by all to the use of the productive factors and to the fruits of co-operation. The labor movement will continue to serve as a reminder of the social responsibilities and duties of government and business. Day-to-day struggles of workers and peasants will continue to exert a progressive influence upon the national economy; for "the social condition of labor in any country is an index of its progress and civilization" and "the just and equitable solution of social problems is the real test of the efficiency of democracy to meet present-day conditions."

For a long time to come, the Philippines will probably remain the "vintage where the grapes of wrath are stored." Organized labor is an important element in the realization of President Quezon's national ambition, "that the Philippines shall become a country where poverty is unknown, and where justice is the watchword, and democracy and freedom the motto." The pressure of organized labor alone may not be able to keep the country on the path of progress, but it can contribute greatly to that end.

BIBLIOGRAPHY

OFFICIAL DOCUMENTS AND REPORTS

Labor Bulletin, issued by the Division of Labor Statistics, Department of Labor, Manila

The Philippine Statistical Review, issued by the Department of Agriculture, Manila, 1934

The Fact-Finding Survey (unpublished), Department of Labor, Manila, 1935

Annual Report, Department of Labor, Manila, 1937

Facts and Figures about the Philippines, Department of Agriculture and Commerce, Manila, 1939

The Census of the Philippines, Bureau of the Census, Manila, 1939

Yearbook of Philippine Statistics, 1940, Manila, 1941

BOOKS

DURAN, P. *Philippine Independence and the Far Eastern Question,* Manila, 1935

HAYDEN, J. R. *The Philippines, A Study in National Development,* New York, 1942

LASKER, B. *Filipino Immigration,* Chicago, 1932

MALCOLM, G. A. *The Commonwealth of the Philippines,* New York, 1936

MITCHELL, KATE, ed. *Industrialization of the Western Pacific,* New York, 1942

PORTER, CATHERINE. *Crisis in the Philippines,* New York, 1942

SMITH, R. A. Our Future in Asia, New York, 1940

MONOGRAPHS

LAVA, H. C. *Levels of Living in the Ilocos Region,* Philippine Council, Institute of Pacific Relations, Manila, 1938

LEAGUE FOR THE DEFENSE OF DEMOCRACY, *The Agrarian Problem,* Manila, 1938

RUNES, I. T. *General Standards of Living and Wages of Workers in the Philippine Sugar Industry,* Philippine Council, Institute of Pacific Relations, Manila, 1939

PERIODICAL ARTICLES

ALLEN, J. S. "Who Owns the Philippines?" *The Nation,* New York, April 24, 1937

AQUINO, E. "Philippine Economic Objectives," *Business,* Manila, November 1938

ANONYMOUS. "A Philippine Middletown," *Philippine Magazine,* Manila, June 1939

AVELINO, J. "Labor and the Commonwealth," *The Philippines*, Washington, D.C., February, 1941

BALMACEDA, C. "The Co-operative Movement in the Philippines," *The Co-operator*, Manila, June 1939

BUENAVENTURA, T. "Looking Ahead," *The Critic*, Manila, July 15, 1935

BUENSUCESO, B. "The Producer-Consumer Economy," *The Vanguard*, Manila, November 1939

————. "Is Sugar Sweeter than Independence?" *The Vanguard*, Manila, October 1939

CAMUS, J. S. "Early History of Philippine Agriculture," *Report No. 1 of the National Research Council of the Philippines*, Manila, 1935

CAPADOCIA, G. "Strike — The Workers' Only Weapon," *The Vanguard*, Manila, March 1939

CLEMENTE, C. "The Administration Tax Measures," *The Vanguard, Manila*, July 1938

————. "The Economic Conditions of the Philippines—1938," *Kalayan*, Manila, July 15, 1939

FRANCISCO, S. A. "Tuberculosis," *Journal of the Philippine Medical Association*, Manila, September 1938

GUERRERO, I. P. "President Quezon and the Workers' Welfare," *The Vanguard*, Manila, February 1398

————. "Misleaders of Labor," *The Vanguard*, Manila, September 1938

GARMA, E. G. "Philippine Women at the Wheels of Industry," *Commerce*, Manila, November 1938

HESTER, E. D. "Footnotes to Philippine Economics," *Philippine Social Science Review*, Manila, May 1940

HILARIO, J. F. "Inside the Philippines," *The National Review*, Manila, April 30, 1937

JARDELEZA, M. L. "Cost of Medical Care for Laborers," *Journal of Philippine Medical Association*, Manila, December 1938

KURIHARA, K. K. "Economic Nationalism in the Philippines," *Philippine Social Science Review*, Manila, May 1940

LANSANG, J. A. "Quezon's Challenge to Labor," *The Vanguard*, Manila, June 1938

————. "Labor's Divided House," *Herald Mid-Week Magazine*, Manila, July 6, 1938

LOPEZ, R. "To My Fellow Hacenderos," *National Review*, Manila, April 23, 1937

MABBUN, P. M. "The Place of Farmers' Co-operatives in Our National Economy," *Philippine Social Science Review*, Manila, May 1940

MONTELIBANO, R. "Socialism Is Possible in the Philippines," *Socialism Today*, Manila, May 1937

MORALES, M. N. "The Industrial Physician," *Journal of the Philippine Medical Association*, Manila, May 1939

PANGANIBAN, C. "Labor—A Menace or a Hope?" *The Vanguard*, Manila, February 1939

POND, H. B. "U.S.–P.I. Reciprocal Preferences Should Continue," *Business*, Manila, November 1938

RAMIREZ, P. B. "Health Insurance," *Journal of the Philippine Medical Association*, Manila, November 1938

ROYAL INSTITUTE OF INTERNATIONAL AFFAIRS. "The Philippines in Transition," *Bulletin of International News*, London, August 23, 1941

SACAY, F. M. "The Role of the Subsistence Farmstead in Rural Reconstruction," *Philippine Agriculturalist*, March 1940

SANTA ANA, PILAR. "The Emancipation of Women," *National Review*, Manila, March 12, 1937

SANTILLAN, J. "Social Justice—and Our Injured Laborers," *Journal of the Philippine Medical Association*, Manila, August 1938

SANTOS, PEDRO A. "Bill for Agriculture," *Commonwealth Fortnightly*, Manila, March 1937

SMITH, O. "Industrial Compensation Law and Emergency Law Considerations," *Journal of the Philippine Medical Association*, Manila, April 1939

SNOW, E. "Filipinos Change Their Minds," *Asia*, September 1939

TORRES, R. "Our Labor Conditions," *Progressive Farming*, Manila, September 1937

TRINIDAD, M. K. "Secretary Roxas and the Unemployed," *The Vanguard*, Manila, January 1940

———. "Land for the Landless," *National Review*, Manila, March 5, 1937

VAK, S. P. "Human Rights *vs.* Property Rights," *The Vanguard*, Manila, September 1939

INDEX

Accidents, industrial, 50–54
Agrarian reforms, 5, 85–86
Agriculture, 5–6
Agricultural and Industrial Bank, 8
American democracy, 73, 90
American influence: on the labor movement, 61; on standards of living, 42; on status of women, 19; on trade-unionism, 61; on working hours, 49
American protection, 13, 32
Anak Pawis (Sons of Sweat), 72
Apostol, José, Professor, 12
Aquino, Benigno, Secretary of Agriculture and Commerce, 34
Avelino, José, Secretary of Labor, 22

Benitez, Conrado, Dean, University of the Philippines, 21
Bonifacio, Andres, 60
Business "pressure groups," 50

Capital-goods industries, 35
Capital investments, 11–14
Capadocia, Guillermo, General Secretary of the Communist party, 27
Cárdenas, Lazaro, President of Mexico, 24
Child labor, 19, 20, 21
Clemente, C., 40
Collective Bargaining Law (Commonwealth Act No. 183), 25, 64
Collective farming, 86
Collective Labor Movement: control of radical and liberal unions, 74; largest registered union, 71; membership, 76; opposition to, 77; origin, 75–76; presidium, 27, 76; struggle with right-wing unions, 80
Commerce, Bureau of, 36
Commonwealth Government, inauguration of, 64; program of Social Justice, 2
Commonwealth, favoring permanent under American protection, 32, 71 n.
Communists: attitude toward the Social Justice Program, 27; joint resolution, 74, 75; as labor leaders, 77; merger with Socialists, 78; opposition to, 77

Communist-Socialist influence, 72
Company unions, 72
Confederated Workers' Alliance, 74
Consumers' co-operatives, 86
Co-operative experiments, 48, 85, 86
Court of Industrial Relations: settlement of industrial disputes, 65; strike ruling, 67; wage ruling, 43
Cristobal, Ruperto S., 74

de los Reyes, Isabelo, 61
Democracy: American, 73, 90; economic, 91; political, first, 91
Disputes, tenant and industrial, 65

Economic nationalism, 33
Education, 21, 69
Eight-hour law, 25, 49, 50, 62, 87
Evangelista, Crisanto, supreme Communist leader, 74
Export enterprises, 10

Factory inspection, 54
Farm hands, 45
Farm income, 47
Farmers' unions, 71
Filipino women, 19, 20, 21
Foreign capital: control of, 13; direct investments, 11, 12; postwar prospects, 14
Foreign trade: balance of, 13; imports and exports, 10; preferential relations with the United States, 30, 32; relations with the world, 33
Francisco, Dr. S. A., 48
Free trade, 9, 29

Ganap party, 73
General Workers' Union, 27, 72, 86
Geographical setting, 2
Great Depression, 29, 39, 62, 65

Hacienda system, 7
Health, Bureau of, 37, 38, 52
Health insurance, 49–50
Hester, E. D., Economic Adviser to the United States High Commissioner, 33, 41
Hours of work, 49, 50
Housing program, 54–55

95